ARCHITECTURE
IN THE
COWBOY STATE,
1849-1940

A GUIDE

ARCHITECTURE IN THE COWBOY STATE, 1849-1940

A GUIDE

EILEEN F. STARR

with foreword by
David Kathka

Photographs by
Richard Collier

Drawings by
*Jamie Wells and
Herbert E. Dawson*

HIGH PLAINS PRESS
GLENDO, WYOMING

This book is dedicated to my parents,
H. Paul and Eileen D. Starr,
for their continued support
of my interest in historic preservation
and their unflagging encouragement and love.

Library of Congress Cataloging-in-Publication Data

Starr, Eileen F., 1953-
   Architecture in the cowboy state, 1849-1940: a guide

Eileen F. Starr;
foreword by David Kathka;
photographs by Richard L. Collier;
drawings by Jamie Wells and Herbert E. Dawson.
p. cm.
Includes bibliographical references and index.

1. Architecture—Wyoming—Guide-books.
2. Architecture, Modern—19th century—Wyoming—
Guide-books.
3. Architecture, Modern—20th century—Wyoming—
Guide-books.
4. Historic Buildings—Wyoming—Guide-books.
I. Title.

NA730.W8S73 1992   720'.9787—dc   2092-4701
ISBN 0-931271-07-X (pbk.)

Funding for this publication came from three sources:
the Wyoming Historic Preservation Office,
Division of Parks and Cultural Resources,
Department of Commerce;
the National Endowment for the Arts;
and the National Park Service.

This book was produced with aid from
the National Endowment for the Arts.

This publication has also been financed in part with federal
funds from the National Park Service, Department of
Interior. However, the contents and opinions do not
necessarily reflect the views or policies of the
Department of Interior.

The State Historic Preservation Office receives federal
funds from the National Park Service. Regulations of the
U. S. Department of the Interior strictly prohibit unlawful
discrimination in departmental federally assisted programs
on the basis of race, color, national origin, age or handicap.
Any person who believes he or she has been discriminated
against in any program, activity, or facility operated by a
recipient of federal assistance should write to:
Director, Equal Opportunity Program,
U.S. Department of the Interior, National Park Service,
P.O. Box 37127, Washington, D.C. 20013-7127.

◊

Manufactured in the United States of America.

HIGH PLAINS PRESS
539 CASSA ROAD
GLENDO, WYOMING 82213

C O N T E N T S

Town Hall, Dixon, Carbon County.
The Dixon town hall makes use of ornamental concrete block. Montgomery Ward and other merchandisers sold the equipment to make ornamental concrete blocks that resembled stone.

The American West is often referred to as if it constitutes a single, homogeneous region, but in fact there are many American Wests. Joel Garreau, in his book about the numerous "nations" making up the North American continent, divides the American West into several subregions. A number of writers and historians argue that the primary characteristic of the region is its aridity, but arid does not accurately describe western Oregon or Washington. The American West has also been described as a colony of the East, but California certainly no longer fits that description. The American West is then many Wests, and studying its individual parts without the use of stereotypes better enables us to understand the whole.

Eileen Starr's study of Wyoming architecture strips away the myths, the Hollywood images, and provides the reader with an accurate picture of one part of the American West. Starr dispels myths about the "look" of the West that have led over time to misunderstandings and inaccurate stereotypes. She replaces those false images with true stories about the role of ethnic groups, varied businesses and industries, and the ups and downs of the economy in creating contemporary Wyoming. In this book Starr demonstrates not only the practical nature of Wyoming builders, but also the whimsy that sometimes shaped Wyoming's built environment. She also notes how the cowboy myth has been incorporated into the appearance of towns like Jackson, Wyoming, to give the tourists what they expect.

Architecture as an art form—high art as well as folk art—has largely been ignored by historians of the American West. Major texts totally ignore architecture in the West. This failure to come to grips with the architecture of the American West stems from a lack of sources more than from a failure to understand architecture's importance in the history of the region.

Eileen Starr's history of Wyoming architecture shows Wyoming citizens transporting their cultural baggage from Europe and the East Coast of the United States to Wyoming. But it also shows them adapting to their Wyoming environment. This book examines architecture designed by professional architects, and it shows architecture "designed" by common people. Starr looks at buildings that make use of indigenous material as well as buildings that were purchased from catalogs and shipped in by rail. Starr's study helps us to understand that there is much more to Wyoming architecture than false fronts.

The social history of Wyoming is reflected in the architecture of the state. From the architecture of a place we can come away better understanding its class structure and its way of governing, educating, and worshipping. The architecture of Wyoming helps to show how Wyoming is both like other places yet is also very different.

Finally, this book is more than history, more than illustration of art. In the hands of an interested reader, this book can also become a tool for the preservation of Wyoming's heritage because the book also explains how Wyoming architecture might be preserved for the education and enjoyment of future generations.

This is an important book—a book that will contribute to a better understanding of this place we call Wyoming. We hope you enjoy it. We hope you learn from it.

DAVID KATHKA
STATE HISTORIC PRESERVATION OFFICER

Casper Women's Club House, Casper, Natrona County.
The Casper Women's Club House is an architecturally interesting building with detailed terra cotta ornamentation.

This book is written from a preservationist's perspective. Its purpose is to offer Wyoming citizens information on the state's historic architecture with the hope that this will assist and encourage historic preservation efforts. Wyoming's historic buildings are the most visible link to the state's fascinating past: ranches document the importance of agriculture, downtown Rock Springs visually communicates the significance of coal mining, while places such as Jeffrey City and Manville explain the precarious nature of Wyoming's extractive industries. These visible links offer insight into the successes and failures of the past and can offer insight into the future of Wyoming.

Throughout the following pages, I present some general ways to observe and interpret Wyoming's architecture constructed before 1940. This book is an overview, a general analysis of Wyoming's historic architecture, and as such it has the strengths and weaknesses of a broad survey. Perhaps the book could be considered a starting point for the study of Wyoming's architecture; I hope it stimulates other work in the field. In an effort to examine various types of Wyoming's historic architecture, I use the words architect-designed, manufactured and folk to clarify the different design processes that were part of the construction process. Wyoming's architecture is also discussed from a thematic viewpoint (eg. agricultural, commercial, military, recreational architecture). Historic preservation efforts and their role in Wyoming are discussed in chapter six. Finally in the second part of the book, there are guidelines for writing architectural descriptions. Examples of architectural descriptions are included to assist the reader. I hope the reader gleans from the text and illustrations that architect-designed, manufactured and folk architecture are all important pieces of Wyoming's past, and a variety of the state's buildings deserve to be preserved.

Choosing photographs was a challenging task. Hundreds of sites were considered but lack of space prevented the inclusion of many significant buildings. Lack of mention in this publication should not be interpreted as lack of significance. Some important buildings could not be included, and there are types of buildings that are significant but were also excluded due to lack of space.

The illustrations used in the book show buildings that possess a high degree of integrity, structures that remain relatively unchanged, since these buildings easily communicate necessary information. Numerous buildings were considered for this publication but some were hard to photograph because that precious Wyoming commodity, trees, sometimes obscure the state's oldest architecture. For example, the house at the Swan Land and Cattle Company in Chugwater is an excellent example of residential Gothic Revival architecture, but vegetation prevented a clear view of the property. The illustrations focus on historic buildings that are still standing. Since this book is meant to encourage the preservation of existing buildings, there are no historical photographs used to document lost structures.

Unfortunately, only the exterior of buildings will be discussed. It is beyond the scope of this study to examine the interiors of Wyoming's buildings, although examining interiors is key to understanding use patterns and other invaluable aspects of social history. I realize that this lack of interior analysis and interior plans may disappoint some. It was somewhat frustrating for me to limit the study to exteriors.

Wyoming's diverse architectural landscape deserves future study. I hope this publication, written for the general public, encourages further study.

ACKNOWLEDGMENTS

This book is a collaborative work and I owe thanks to many people and agencies.

Due largely to the efforts of Mark Junge, the State Historic Preservation Office (SHPO) has a substantial collection of 4 X 5 negatives that document the state's historic buildings. This collection was an invaluable resource for the book. Staff photographers such as Richard Collier continue to add to the collection.

Richard Collier, Jamie Wells, Diane Cole, and Herbert Dawson all contributed substantially to this book. Richard Collier's expertise with the State Historic Preservation Office's 4 x 5 format Sinar camera is clearly illustrated. Collier's continued willingness to find the best photographs for publication was commendable. The photographs were taken by Collier unless another photographer is specifically credited in the caption. Jamie Wells's line drawings of both buildings and architectural details highlight her passion for historic preservation and her artistic skill. Wells's continued patience and assistance was laudable. Actually this publication was started at a meeting held between then Colorado State Professor Nancy Goodman, Jamie Wells and me.

While Herb Dawson was Historical Architect for our office, he drew four outstanding line drawings for the book. Diane Cole, as a graduate student, assisted with historic research efforts long after her original commitment.

Support for the publication came from many different quarters. David Kathka, State Historic Preservation Officer, and Thomas Marceau, former Deputy State Historic Preservation Officer, were both supportive and helpful. Three colleagues read each draft and patiently offered suggestions for improvement: Wyoming Folk Arts Coordinator Timothy Evans, State Historic Preservation Office Planning Coordinator Rheba Massey and consultant Rose Wagner; their help was invaluable. My sister, Donna Starr, also read drafts and offered editorial suggestions.

Current and former State Historic Preservation Office personnel including Sheila Bricher-Wade, Chris Hall, Mark Junge, Josie Kantner, Kathy Murphy, and Tracy Williams, along with other SHPO staff members, were supportive in a variety of ways. Edith Miller, the patron saint of Wyoming's historic preservation fiscal system, was always cheerful and helpful. Former preservation administrators Robert Bush and Sharon Bollinger lent their support during their tenure with the State of Wyoming. Wyoming's historic preservation commissions, all thirteen of them, each assisted this project in their own way. By surveying historic resources in their communities, the State Historic Preservation Office has learned a great deal about Wyoming's architecture. Under the auspices of the Certified Local Government Program administered by the SHPO, communities have documented ranches, military sites, commercial and residential architecture.

Additionally de Teel Patterson Tiller of the National Park Service and Jan Jennings of Iowa State University reviewed early drafts; their critiques were invaluable. Thomas Wilsted of Wyoming's American Heritage Center assisted the overall effort by allowing us to photograph parts of the Montgomery Ward collection. Gloria Anderson of the *Wyoming Eagle/Tribune* provided access to some of the architectural advertisements. Documenting the work of Wyoming's architects was made easier by the assistance of William Dubois and Elinor Hitchcock Mullens. Mabel Brown also helped document Newcastle's buildings. The editorial skill and Wyoming historical knowledge of Nancy Curtis, High Plains Press, were essential to the project.

My friends and family were the most supportive of all; their continued interest and help made this project possible.

Funding for the publication came from three different sources: the National Endowment for the Arts, the National Park Service, and the State of Wyoming's financial support to the Wyoming State Historic Preservation Office. The initial grant from the National Endowment for the Arts actually made the project feasible. Many thanks to the NEA, NPS and the State of Wyoming. I feel very fortunate I was given the opportunity to write about Wyoming's architecture.

Left—
*Carter Hotel False Front,
Carter, Uinta County.*
The Carter Hotel is a
typical frame false front
with minimal ornamental
detail and a substantial
parapet wall that makes
the hotel appear larger
than it actually is.

CHAPTER ONE

The Western Myth and Architecture

To many, "Wyoming" is synonymous with one of America's favorite stories—the legend of the Wild West and its cowboys. Historically, Wyoming's architecture has been influenced by the livestock industry and the cattleman's way of life. However, an equally dominant force is the myth of the cowboy, perpetuated first by the dime novel and later by motion pictures and television.

Virtually all Americans have grown up immersed in the cowboy legend. It's a familiar tale—the strong, weather-beaten man who works hard, takes care of himself and his loved ones, and when confronted with evil, overcomes the intruder. Ultimately, this hero is rewarded for his efforts, the agrarian ideal is restored and evil is dispelled. It's a great story which makes life seem much simpler than it actually is. Perhaps, the legend represents how people would like life to be.

Left—Cowboy Bar, Jackson, Teton County.
Both the interior and exterior of the Cowboy Bar express the Hollywood cowboy myth. The bucking bronc neon sign towers over the gnarled log exterior. Inside, saddles serve as the seats of bar stools.

And perhaps that is why the image and the story are so appealing.

Americans are so fascinated with the cowboy myth that the symbol has become ubiquitous. In Wyoming, you'll find Cowboy Motors, athletic teams nicknamed the Cowboys and the Cowgirls, bucking broncos on the state license plates, and countless Cowboy Bars.

Wyoming and other Rocky Mountain states are all participants in the myth that defines or characterizes the West. Several sources helped initiate and then perpetuate the western myth. Novels produced around the turn of the century, such as Owen Wister's *The Virginian*, conveyed the image of the strong, silent cowboy. Buffalo Bill's Wild West Show traveled throughout the United States and Europe bringing staged theatrical battles to thousands who watched "conflicts" between Native Americans and the military, as well as demonstrations of cowboy skills such as roping, riding, and shooting.

Hollywood's cowboy movies cultivated the western image by portraying the frontier as an action-packed adventureland where good and evil constantly confronted each other. Sometimes

Hollywood offered rather erroneous views of western life. One classic and fanciful example is the singing cowboy made famous by Gene Autry and Roy Rogers. Yet, during the thirties and forties the handsome cowboy riding his horse with a guitar in his hand, singing to the cattle on the wide-open range was an image widely viewed and enjoyed. Fanciful ideas concerning western architecture were also seen on motion picture screens by millions of people.

The television West, brought into our living rooms by popular programs like *Gunsmoke* and *Bonanza,* relayed certain visual myths about western settlements. Western towns were portrayed as "boom and bust" colonies, places with no permanence that were established yesterday, but could be vacant tomorrow. Frequently the buildings in these television towns were frame, two-story structures with misshapen false fronts. Elaborate Victorian ornaments decorated some structures, but the buildings were so poorly constructed that the cowboy hero could easily throw the villain in the black hat through a wall or a window. Every television frontier settlement had boardwalks which echoed under the heels of the deputy's boots as he made his nightly rounds.

The subtle message that Hollywood delivered was that the architecture of the West was odd and impermanent. And in comparison to the action-packed adventures, western buildings were unimportant.

When Americans are asked what architectural image best represents the West, they frequently respond with "the false front." Actually, false-fronted buildings were constructed throughout the entire United States during the nineteenth century and not just in the West. But probably due to Hollywood settings, many Americans perceive the false front to be the building of the West.

False fronts really were among the first type of buildings to be constructed in new towns in Wyoming territory. Along with tents and crude log cabins, frame false front buildings were built because they were easily constructed and inexpensive. The large parapet wall, which is the identifier of a false front, towered over the street and gave the building a look of prosperity that could not be achieved with a tent or small log cabin. But, in essence, there was nothing behind the parapet wall; hence the name—the false front.

Dance Hall, New Fork, Sublette County.
The New Fork Dance Hall, originally called the Valhalla Dance Hall, was constructed in 1909 for the settlement of New Fork. Most false fronts in Wyoming are not quite this ornate. The dance hall is still used for community dances.

Since prosperity was rarely assured in a boom town, the false front was an image with literally nothing behind it. The false front building represented the merchant's or builder's hopes for the future. In a way, these authentic nineteenth-century false fronts are some of the earliest stage sets of the West—buildings designed to appear to be something they were not, buildings designed to represent a false reality. Perhaps that is why Hollywood set designers felt such an affinity toward the false front as a symbol of western architecture.

In actuality, frame false fronts were quickly replaced with buildings constructed of more durable stone and brick when the property owner could afford something more substantial. Today it is unusual to find a frame false front in any of Wyoming's urban areas, although some do still stand in Wyoming's smaller towns.

Wyoming's identification with the image of the false front and the cowboy is so strong and the legend so entrenched that architects used the symbol on their buildings sixty years ago. Visitors to Cheyenne's Frontier Hotel, built in 1936, are greeted by a large, friendly-looking terra cotta cowboy. Cowboys and Native Americans,

Frontier Hotel, Cheyenne, Laramie County.
The ornamental detail on the hotel, built in 1936, supposedly depicts Frontier Days Bronc Riding Champion, Pete Knight. The cowboy medallion is terra cotta and tipis surround the sides of the medallion.

Steer head, Dubois, Fremont County. A commercial enterprise in Dubois captures tourists' attention with an oversized steer head which frames an entry. The steer head is not historic but is a modern display of the importance of the cowboy myth to Wyoming.

sodbusters and emigrants, and even an oil well are carved into the Indiana limestone of the Natrona County Courthouse. When Casper architects Karl Krusmark and Leon Goodrich designed the courthouse in 1940 as part of a Public Works Administration project, they placed a miniature version of Wyoming's history in sculpture along the top of the building. Moreover, Dubois, Wyoming, has an unusual steer head that frames an entryway; the steer's head reputedly travels from one commercial building to another along the strip northwest of town. Although not historic, it is a creative piece of roadside architecture. These architectural representations of Wyoming's cowboy culture document the state's fondness for its agricultural heritage, both the reality and the myth.

Myths and symbols have their place. However, unfortunately, through the years Hollywood images seem to have replaced traditional sources, such as historic photographs, as the basis for information about buildings and history. Often when a town decides to promote tourism, the idea of "westernizing" is discussed. To "westernize" a town, one must create board sidewalks,

put up a hitching rail to tie horses to, and construct frame false fronts on the top of existing buildings. The sad result is historic storefronts covered with someone's idea of what the town looked like when it was an insecure boom town. Using popular, but misconceived, visual images as sources for correct architectural information leads to chaotic construction which is not representative of any western town which ever existed anyplace other than on a Hollywood stage set.

Although many recreated frontier settlements are not architecturally accurate, they must be recognized as commercial successes. Jackson, Wyoming, continues to market that myth of the West. New buildings are constructed to look "western." Some buildings in downtown Jackson are actually historic, such as the stone drugstore and the Cowboy Bar. Many of the buildings built during the last ten years around the town square were designed to capture the tourists' eyes as well as their money. But most modern tourists are sophisticated enough to recognize the difference between authentic historic buildings and an artificial commercial area. What works in Jackson is largely due to the continuing influx of tourists in search of beautiful scenery and unsurpassed recreational opportunities who are willing to suspend historic reality and step into a theme-park-styled Frontierland.

In Wyoming, interest continues in developing and marketing the Hollywood myth for tourists' dollars. For example, new buildings constructed

Natrona County Courthouse, Casper, Natrona County.
Important themes in Wyoming's history are characterized by figures carved into limestone on this courthouse. The Works Progress Administration paid for construction of the courthouse in 1940. Local architects Karl Krusmark and Leon Goodrich created a highly imaginative design.

Territorial Prison Park, Laramie, Albany County. Recently constructed false front buildings at the Territorial Prison Park are used to convey a feeling of the "Old West."

at the Territorial Prison Park complex in Laramie were designed to emulate nineteenth-century boom town architecture. Obviously, the designers were driven by commercial and economic concerns as well as by educational goals. The false fronts and canvas buildings at the Territorial Prison are intended to evoke a spirit or feeling for the past. Yet the false front designs are not accurate representations of Wyoming false fronts; the proportions and massing of the new false fronts are misrepresented. The entire "settlement" would have looked as odd and out of place in the 1870s as it does today situated along Interstate 80. In contrast, Albany County and Laramie are rich sources of authentic western architecture, that if preserved and interpreted for the public, would result in a far more valuable historical asset than a "westernized" Hollywood image of an inaccurate past. Admittedly, however, the cowboy myth is wrapped with a magnetic aura that draws tourists and their dollars with a power which historic preservation seems to lack.

There is much more to Wyoming's historic architecture than false fronts and wooden sidewalks. Cowboys and our agricultural past are

significant parts of the state's history and made contributions to its architecture, but they are not the only part of the past. Wyoming has an interesting and diverse history and culture. Scandinavians built intricate log barns, the railroads produced formidable depots, and the oil industry constructed a highly unusual company town at Sinclair.

Fortunately, Wyoming has hundreds of noteworthy historic buildings that retain their original appearance and deserve our respect and protection. This book provides a sampling of Wyoming's historic architecture with the text and pictures. Wyoming's historic architecture is the most visible manifestation of the state's history and is well worth preserving.

Territorial Prison Park, Laramie, Albany County. Promoters of the park created an interpretation of a nineteenth-century boom town, in addition to rehabilitating the old prison.

Left—
Holy City, Park County.
Rock pinnacles along the north fork of the Shoshone River conveyed architectural qualities to early settlers. They named the formation "Holy City."

Architecture: Landscape and Culture

The topography of Wyoming is one of sharp contrasts: jagged glaciated peaks, dusty desert areas, and rolling grasslands are all part of the scene. Climactic conditions such as the lack of water and the ubiquitous wind are common links among each of the geologic phenomenon—the mountains, high plains, and basins. Each of these geologically distinct areas offered natural building materials to the first settlers in the form of stone outcroppings, glacial moraines, and forested hillsides; all were rich organic resources during the nineteenth and twentieth centuries.

Bewildered by the wide open spaces and looking for the comfort of home, nineteenth-century travelers believed that Wyoming's natural rock formations resembled buildings. Perhaps due to the uncomfortable nature of travel during the middle of the nineteenth century, emigrants

Left—Castle Rock, Green River, Sweetwater County. The historic Sweetwater Brewery building incorporates some of the architectural qualities associated with the rock formation towering in the background, Castle Rock. *(photo by Clayton Fraser.)*

traveling along the Oregon Trail used their memories of previous places to name unusual geologic features located along the trail. A large, layered rock structure that towers over an area along the Green River was named "Castle Rock." Settlers in the Wapiti Valley in Park County found architectural qualities expressed in the sculpted volcanic rock pinnacles along the north fork of the Shoshone River and named the area "Holy City." Wyoming's architecture, either carved from natural landscape formations or constructed by man,

has always had a strong link to the surrounding environment.

Some of the first white settlers used the land to their advantage by employing a hillside for constructing a shelter or using a stone wall to protect their newborn calves. The Stone Wall Ranch in southern Carbon County illustrates how part of a large stone wall was integrated into the corral system to protect livestock from the elements.

Other settlers used hillsides for sheltering humans by excavating a hole inside the earth to

Stone Wall Ranch, Carbon County.
Ranchers took advantage of the solid barricade and natural protection provided by this stone ledge by integrating it into the corral system. The stone wall provides some protection for newborn calves.

Dugout, Campbell County.
Settlers literally dug out a
hillside to create shelter.
This Campbell County
dugout is rather elaborate
with its stone wall
supports.

form a shelter called a dugout. Generally, dugouts were considered temporary housing until something more substantial could be constructed, such as a log or frame cabin.

The builders of the Anderson Lodge located in the Washakie Wilderness area in Park County logically used logs to construct their shelter because trees were a resource that was readily available in 1890. Others used stone, sod or different types of accessible materials.

Buildings must be evaluated for architectural importance in the context of the surrounding neighborhood, landscape, and region because both the geography and the building's form offer important information about the past. Architecture cannot be divorced from its surroundings.

ARCHITECTURE AND CULTURE Architecture is influenced by a variety of factors including purpose, climate, technological developments of the age, availability of construction materials, and the cultural background of the builder. Of all the determinants that influence the construction of a building, one of the strongest factors is the cultural and social background of the builder.

Anderson Lodge, Park County. Local materials were used to construct the Anderson Lodge. Located in the Shoshone National Forest, access to the lodge is limited to horse or foot traffic. The building has saddle-notched corners, as well as saddles on the hitching rail.

Sturgis House, Laramie County. Constructed in 1884 for a wealthy cattleman, the Sturgis House is reputedly one of the first houses in the West to be constructed in the "shingle style." Architects George Rainsford and W.A. Bates designed the house.

People have always drawn upon their previous experiences to help define what form and plan to use when constructing a new building. For example, during the seventeenth century, the colonists in Jamestown, Virginia, decided to build brick townhouses similar to those in England; although the settlers had a vast amount of land to utilize, they built tight rows of houses that reminded them of their former homeland. Much later in time, when people moved to Wyoming, they too used forms that were familiar to those of their cultural group. For example, Scandinavians working as tie hacks (loggers who carved railroad ties from Wyoming's pines for the railroads) built cabins that were similar to the ones they left in Europe.

Buildings reflect the intellectual thoughts and aesthetic ideas that were popular and acceptable when the structures were built. Builders were as socially conscious during past centuries as they are today; how a building would be received by others has always been a factor in determining its appearance. Architects George Rainsford and W. A. Bates designed an elegant residence covered with shingles for cattle baron William Sturgis in 1884. The house, located in Cheyenne, is similar to New England shingle style residences built during the late nineteenth century. It is reputedly one of the first examples of a home covered with shingles constructed in the Rocky Mountain West. The architects chose the shingle style because it was considered fashionable during the 1880s.

Greek Orthodox Church of Saints Constantine and Helen, Cheyenne, Laramie County. The architectural elements in this church display its ethnic origins.

Woods Landing Dance Hall, Albany County. The historic Woods Landing Dance Hall was constructed by Scandinavian Hokum Lestum in 1932. The dance hall displays its Scandinavian origins in the distinctive corner treatment.

In some areas, architecture instantly communicates the ethnic background of its builders. Typically ethnic connections are easier to distinguish in religious or fraternal architecture. Some churches obviously indicate their association with a particular culture, such as Cheyenne's Greek Orthodox Church of Saints Constantine and Helen with its towers, windows, gilding and overall appearance. Wyoming's ethnic architecture may be slightly harder to recognize than in some other parts of the country. Of course, ethnic diversity does indeed exist in Wyoming.

Scandinavians constructed log buildings in many sections of Wyoming. The Woods Landing Dance Hall, constructed by Hokum Lestum, has strong characteristics of typical Scandinavian

Sodergren Barn, Albany County. The full dovetail notching at the corners of the Sodergren barn, as well as the interior stalls, are excellent examples of the high level of craftsmanship in Wyoming's Scandinavian buildings.

Manville Grocery, Manville, Niobrara County.
The "boom and bust" syndrome is evident in this building constructed in the earlier part of the twentieth century to serve the Lance Creek Oil Field workers. Oil was discovered at Lance Creek in 1917, and the Lance Creek field was the largest producer of oil in Wyoming from 1939-1945. When the bust came, the population plummeted. Many buildings at Manville were demolished over the years and only foundations remain.

construction, demonstrated by the peeled round logs, the manner in which the logs fit together and the stepped notched corners. Yet unless an observer is familiar with the history of the area or Scandinavian construction techniques, the ethnic associations of the dance hall are not obvious.

Wyoming's boom and bust history is also evident in its architecture. Construction materials added to houses in Rock Springs illustrate the flush and lean times. Aluminum and asbestos siding often covered "old fashioned" wood cladding when owners could afford to update their houses. When the inevitable bust came, sometimes property owners were forced to sell buildings inexpensively or chose to demolish structures rather than pay property taxes. Towns that once had a more prosperous outlook, such as Manville or Jeffrey City, visually indicate the precarious nature of settlements which grow up because of extractive industries.

Architecture is functional as well as being one of the most accessible forms of art; it's an integral component of our everyday lives. Some of Wyoming's buildings are highly decorative while others are frankly utilitarian.

Both landscape and culture influence the type of architecture that is found in Wyoming, as do other determinants. Wyoming's distinctive landscape provides a beautiful setting for the state's diverse historic buildings.

CHAPTER THREE

Interpreting Wyoming's Historic Architecture

Wyoming's historic buildings can be classified in three broad categories: architect- or builder-designed, manufactured, and folk. These categories do not have rigid definitions that classify buildings according to a strict scientific method nor are the categories mutually exclusive. Instead, they offer a general way to view, interpret, and perhaps appreciate, the state's historic architecture.

Architect-designed structures are those structures designed with a specific site and client in mind. Some of the construction materials may have been mass produced while other elements were crafted on site.

In contrast, manufactured architecture refers to buildings that were mass-produced. Plans for manufactured buildings were circulated in newspaper advertisements, in inexpensive plan books, or in design pages available at the local

Left—Motley-Garson Double Barns, Albany County.

These log barns are mirror images of each other, although one was constructed for cattle while the other was reputedly constructed for elk. Double barns are unusual in Wyoming. The elk barn has carefully crafted stalls with swinging doors that provide entry to the front of the stalls. The barns are examples of piece-sur-piece construction, a type of folk architecture found in Wyoming.

lumberyard. The majority of the construction material was mass produced in this category of architecture.

Finally, ideas about construction of buildings in the folk architecture category are shared in a traditional manner from one generation to the next. Builders of folk buildings did not employ architectural plans, and construction materials were usually obtained locally.

ARCHITECT-DESIGNED The student of Wyoming's architecture will observe some buildings which are indeed monumental. These structures possess qualities of design that make them different from ordinary buildings. Monumental buildings designed by architects, and even more modest architect-designed buildings, have been viewed by art historians for decades in terms of "style."

Essentially, architectural style refers to the visual aspects of the building and its overall design and ornamentation. In this book, the concept of style will refer to particular architectural qualities associated with historical periods—such as Classical, Gothic, and Romanesque.

For centuries, builders drew upon former designs and architectural elements to create innovative designs or patterns. Builders intentionally emulated previous times. Particular patterns became associated with different types of architecture. For instance, many American governmental structures, with their classical columns and symmetrical massing, suggest a relationship to the egalitarian values of ancient Greece. This style, known as Neoclassical, served as a model for later designs in which the architect wanted to convey a sense of permanence and stability.

Wyoming's architect-designed buildings illustrate the architectural as well as social philosophy of their day; they even indicate popular fads. The architects of these buildings incorporated state-of-the-art technological advances into their designs. More capital was usually available for the construction of monumental structures than for ordinary buildings, so architect-designed buildings were often monumental in scale compared to other edifices. For the wealthy, architect-designed buildings were a means of expressing their economic standing and place in the community. Governmental structures, fraternal organization

Cooper Mansion, Laramie, Albany County.
Designed by Wilbur Hitchcock, the Cooper Mansion is unlike
any other residence in the state, yet it does not clearly fit
into a specific architectural style category.
(Photo by Doug Goodman.)

Masonic Temple, Laramie, Albany County.
William Dubois designed this Neoclassical building for the Masons. The pediment, ionic columns and overall form of the building is typical of Neoclassical architecture.

buildings, cathedrals, and homes for the upper-middle class or wealthy were frequently designed by architects and were site-specific. Sometimes the architect used locally available materials, but, on occasion, exotic construction materials were imported.

Traditional style terminology offered by architectural historians such as Marcus Whiffen or Leland Roth is useful in describing some of Wyoming's buildings. For example, the previously mentioned Sturgis House in Cheyenne is an excellent display of the shingle style, while the Platte County Courthouse is a Neoclassical structure. Yet, few structures in the state display pure styles; more often they are a combination of styles. Some people have become frustrated with standardized architectural classifications and have invented their own stylistic terminology—such as "high plains commercial" or "victorianetic" or "pagodaesque"—to allow hybrid buildings to be grouped into a category.

Occasionally, architectural historians fail to agree on classifications. When the Cooper Mansion in Laramie was in danger of being demolished, one professional called the building an

"Italian Villa," another referred to it as "Spanish Colonial" and another designated it "Mission Revival." Arguments can be made for each of these designations on the basis of the building's stylistic elements, but the Cooper Mansion is not a pure example of any particular style. Yet, it is the only building of its kind in Wyoming and, therefore, possesses significance even if it cannot be given a specific stylistic title.

Three examples of Wyoming's architect-designed or "high style" facades are Laramie's Masonic Temple, the Cheyenne Union Pacific Depot, and Saint Matthew's Cathedral in Laramie.

A versatile and prolific Cheyenne architect, William Dubois, designed the Laramie Masonic Temple in 1911. Dubois selected the Classical motif because of the Masons' interest in ancient history. The Neoclassical details of the building are immediately apparent; the entire structure resembles a temple from the ancient world. Neoclassical architecture is based upon the architecture of Greece and Rome dating from approximately 600 B.C. to 400 A.D. Ionic columns, symmetrical massing, sparse use of ornamentation, and a pediment adorning the facade are all symbols of the Neoclassic style. Greek temples were constructed from stone and contained some details that differed from those of Laramie's Masonic Temple. Nonetheless, Architect Dubois demonstrated his familiarity with Classical design elements, creating a building with a memorable design.

Henry Van Brunt and Frank Howe, an architectural team from Kansas City, designed the Cheyenne depot for the Union Pacific Railroad in 1886. From an architectural standpoint, the depot is one of the most significant buildings in the Rocky Mountain West. Architect Van Brunt was a tremendously talented nineteenth-century architect as well as a man of letters who wrote a variety of treatises. Stylistically, the structure can be considered Romanesque Revival based upon Romanesque architecture of the eleventh and twelfth centuries. European Romanesque buildings have round arches, large interior vaults, and massive walls decorated with sculpture and architectural ornaments. The continuous use of round arches on the facade, the rough texture of the stonework and the decorative molding, give the depot a Romanesque feel.

Ames Monument, Summit between Laramie and Cheyenne, Albany County.

Henry Hobson Richardson, famous nineteenth-century architect, designed this monument honoring Oliver and Oakes Ames, Union Pacific Railroad promoters. This sixty-foot structure, with the sandstone medallions of the Oakes brothers sculpted by artist Augustus Saint-Gaudens, was completed in 1882 and cost $75,000. (Photo by Liz Stambaugh.)

Some consider the depot Richardsonian Romanesque because of its similarity to the work of Henry Hobson Richardson, a well-known nineteenth-century architect who coincidentally designed the Ames Monument located between Laramie and Cheyenne. Richardson used Romanesque architectural elements and elaborated upon them. Nineteenth-century architects were expected to be well-versed in a number of historical styles and were often skilled enough to design a Gothic Revival church, a Romanesque school, and a Neoclassical government building.

Laramie's Saint Matthew's Cathedral, like many religious structures throughout the United States, can be associated with the the Gothic Revival style. Gothic architecture had its origin in France during the mid-twelfth century. The pointed arch, a hallmark of the style, was used extensively to accent windows and doors and was also used as a decorative motif. Technological developments of the twelfth century such as the flying buttress, which helped transfer the load of the extensive roof and vaulting systems to the ground, are easily observed in Gothic cathedrals in Europe. Richard Upjohn and other

Union Pacific Depot, Cheyenne, Laramie County.
This depot is today one of the most significant depots in the Rocky Mountains. Designed by noted architects Henry Van Brunt and Frank Howe in 1886, the depot's architectural associations are Romanesque Revival.

nineteenth-century architects successfully convinced American patrons that the Gothic Revival style was the academically and historically correct style for churches, schools and other structures. Philosophically, it was believed Gothic architecture exemplified good Christian values.

Saint Matthew's Cathedral was designed by New York City architect William H. Wood, who attempted to meet all the architectural standards for creating a correct Gothic design. The building has a pointed arch encapsulating the double doors, and the pointed arch motif is used to ornament the belfry and spire. The overall massing of the structure in a modified cruciform plan is typical of the Gothic Revival style. Many cathedrals in Europe such as Chartres in France were so intricate that it took craftsmen centuries to finish them. Although Saint Matthew's is not that elaborate, it is still one of the finest examples of Gothic Revival architecture in Wyoming.

Other monumental buildings within the state have their own stylistic origins. Wyoming does not have the diversity of stylistic structures that more populous states have. The lack of capital during settlement, in comparison to gold- and

Left—Saint Matthew's Cathedral, Laramie, Albany County. Saint Matthew's, an Episcopal cathedral, was designed by architect William H. Wood in a Gothic Revival style. Construction of the cathedral began in the 1890s, but the tower remained unfinished until the twentieth century. (*Drawing by Jamie Wells.*)

silver-rich Montana and Colorado, meant that less money was expended for early architect-designed structures. Still, many of the state's buildings have architectural elements derived from established styles.

MANUFACTURED ARCHITECTURE

The majority of Wyoming's historic buildings are examples of manufactured architecture. The primary distinction between architect-designed and manufactured buildings is not the appearance, but rather the design process. Where did the plans come from? Was the design created specifically for a site or was it used repeatedly? In what manner was the structure built? How were the materials acquired? Architect-designed buildings were constructed for a specific site and client, but the vast majority of historic buildings do not meet these criteria. Instead, most are manufactured buildings, products of the nineteenth-century's industrial revolution.

During the nineteenth century, plans for commercial and residential structures were mass produced which allowed a building to be constructed anywhere in the United States. Designs were published in newspapers, plan and pattern books, and magazines of the period. Frequently anonymous architects produced the designs for these mass-produced buildings. A wide variety of simple, as well as some very complex, designs were available to the public as a result of marketing efforts; entire sets of construction drawings could be purchased from firms in other states. To complement the rich diversity of designs, trade catalogs, lumberyards and serials advertised an amazing variety of construction materials which also could be purchased through the mail. An example of interesting manufactured architecture is the highly decorative Ferris Mansion in Rawlins, which was designed by an architectural firm in Knoxville, Tennessee, who made the plans widely available.

The industrial revolution was in full swing when the first permanent settlements in Wyoming grew up along the tracks of the Union Pacific Railroad. Ultimately, the railroad determined what buildings were first constructed in Wyoming. Rail lines provided access to inexpensive, mass-produced construction materials manufactured in the Midwest and also provided

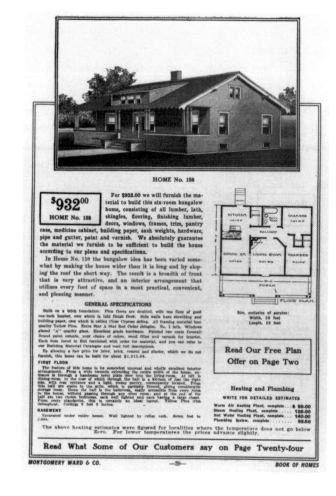

affordable and efficient transportation.

Local lumberyards and builders in Wyoming stocked materials such as molding, windows, doors, and exterior cladding materials that were manufactured in the Midwest and transported to Wyoming by rail. Entire buildings could be purchased through the mail and delivered to Wyoming. Sears, Roebuck and Company was one of several corporations which sold packages that supplied all the exterior and interior materials necessary for the construction of a specific house. Sears even offered interior design suggestions as well as ideas for landscaping. The availability of inexpensive yet attractive housing reinforced the desirability of home ownership, even among citizens of modest means.

Montgomery Ward began selling houses from catalogs around 1910 and continued in the residential mail-order business until the Depression. Houses from Sears and Wards represented popular housing styles of the times.

Houses ordered from Wards came either "ready-cut" or "not ready cut." According to the Wardway Homes catalog of 1918, "A Ready-Cut home can be built in less time, with less skilled

Ferris Mansion, Rawlins, Carbon County.
The design for the Ferris Mansion came from the architectural firm of Barber and Klutz in Tennessee. The decorative mansion illustrates the diversity of housing that was available from pattern books at the turn of the century.

Bungalow near Lost Cabin, Fremont County.
This interesting bungalow, another example of manufactured architecture, has a gable ornament with an Oriental appearance. Bungalows are one of the most common houses found in Wyoming.

labor and at less expense—but in Ready-Cut plans no changes should be made as to size of the building, exterior arrangement of doors, windows or roof line."

Catalog specifications explained exactly what grade and type of materials were included in the package. For example, exterior siding was either clear grade red cedar or cypress, while first and second story windows were constructed of clear white pine. Wards even included a section on "how you can cut cost—climate permitting." The 1918 catalog states, "Remember, we furnish regularly Extra Clear, 5 to 2 Washington Red Cedar Shingles, acknowledged to be the best. We could supply Extra Star A (6 to 2) Red Cedar. These are a thinner shingle and cost less."

Architects of manufactured buildings used the same building forms and plans over and over again. Housing in Wyoming's planned communities such as Parco and Sunrise illustrate the repetitive use of the same building plans.

Over the years, buildings with certain similarities acquired standard names, such as foursquare and bungalow.

At the beginning of the twentieth century, thousands of similar houses, now referred to as

American Foursquares or Prairie Cubes, began to dot the landscape. Two-story, square or rectangular buildings with hipped roofs and limited ornamentation became very popular in middle-class neighborhoods. The foursquare is an enclosed, two-story box with straightforward massing, topped by a prominent cornice and a hipped roof. Architectural details such as molding, porches and doors differ from foursquare to foursquare, but the overall rectilinear character of these buildings remains the same. In comparison to houses of the late nineteenth century, foursquares have a minimum of detail. A one-story porch usually adorns the facade, and a dormer is frequently found on the roof. Exterior cladding material may be either brick, stucco, shingle or novelty siding.

Bungalows, another popular twentieth-century residential form, are found in Wyoming and throughout the United States. The basic form of the bungalow, a one- or one-and-a-half-story, rectangular-shaped structure with a low-pitched roof and prominent eaves, demonstrates a variety of designs. A bungalow in Lost Cabin, Wyoming, shows several influences including those from

Foursquare, Cheyenne, Laramie County.
This example of manufactured architecture is referred to by some as a foursquare, although this building has characteristics of a Colonial Revival house. The name for the foursquare comes from its shape.
(*Drawing by Herbert E. Dawson.*)

Ramrod Gun Shop, Cheyenne, Laramie County.
This commercial building is across the street from the main rail line. Parts of the building—such as the cornice, lintel, and pilasters—were ordered from a catalog. The pilasters that separate each bay bear the name of the manufacturer, Pullis Brothers of St. Louis.

the Orient. The distinctive gable ornament, exaggerated eaves, and the stone piers highlight the facade of this bungalow. As in the case of many Wyoming houses, the materials were delivered to Lost Cabin on the local rail line.

Frequently, commercial buildings were also a product of the manufactured system of construction. Businessmen studied the trade catalogs of eastern or midwestern manufacturers and selected building elements from a wide range of supplies—including entire storefronts, doors and other decorative details. Pullis Brothers of St. Louis manufactured the sheet metal front for the Ramrod Gun Shop in Cheyenne. The sheet metal front, also sometimes referred to as an iron-front, consists of a substantial cornice, a lintel separating the first from the second story, and pilasters or decorative dividers separating windows and doors into distinct bays. The pilasters bear the name of the manufacturer. Commercial facades in Wyoming frequently bear the name of iron manufacturers such as the Mesker Brothers located in the Midwest.

A commercial building in Lovell exhibits stylistic features popular at the turn of the century and also shows what materials could be brought to Lovell by train. The pedimented entry of the building, decorated by a garland and guilloche molding on the primary cornice and dentil work, illustrates how Neoclassical details were integrated into a simple storefront. The entry and the cornice are both fabricated metal pieces readily available to Wyoming builders.

FOLK ARCHITECTURE

Some of Wyoming's most interesting structures display no architect-designed elements or manufactured materials. These intriguing buildings exhibit craftsmanship attained only by man's hand. These buildings fall into the category of folk architecture.

One key word can be used to describe folk architecture—traditional. In this category, ideas concerning the exterior design, the interior plans, the construction techniques, and the preparation of construction materials are passed from one generation to the next by informal methods, usually orally or through hands-on experience.

The design of a folk building is derived from the knowledge of its builder. The structure reflects his background, creativity and level of

Commercial Building, Lovell, Big Horn County.
Manufactured architectural details highlight this commercial building found along the main street in Lovell. The Neoclassical entry and ornamental cornice illustrate the variety of manufactured materials that were available in the Big Horn Basin during the early twentieth century. *(Drawing by Jamie Wells.)*

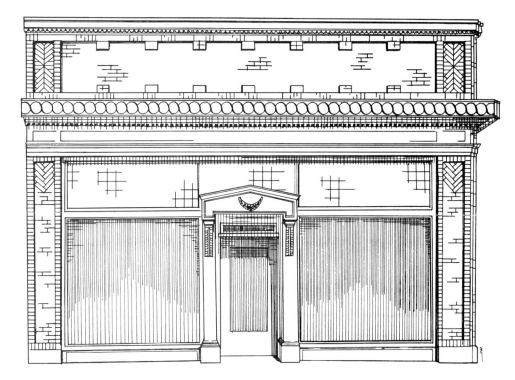

craftsmanship. The design process is informal, and regular architectural plans are not part of the scenario. As in manufactured architecture, repetitive forms or types are seen; however, the builders did not rely on mass-produced plans nor manufactured elements.

The single pen log cabin, a distinctive folk building type, is found both on Wyoming's forested mountains and on the high plains. A "pen," in log house terminology, refers to a unit in which four log walls are fastened together with corner-notching. The single pen cabin is a very simple, rectangular or square, one-story building. Walls are joined by a variety of corner notching types, and the structure is covered with a gable roof. Frequently in Wyoming, the roof was made from sod.

The Nicholas Swan cabin in Sublette County is a good example of a homestead cabin typifying the single pen type. Construction on the fourteen-by-sixteen-foot cabin occurred between 1878 and 1880. Builder Swan used hewn cottonwood logs, joining them with half-dovetail notching. Doors on the east and west sides provided access to the one-room, sod-roofed cabin. Swan was typical of those who built folk structures, in that he directly participated in the construction of his cabin and used locally available native materials, such as stone and logs.

The buildings of an area settled by a particular ethnic or religious group often reflect the background of the settlers. Swedish tie hacks, who cut railroad ties for the transcontinental railroad, brought with them ideas about how to build log cabins. Some Swedes were quite adept at constructing V-notched corners that joined the walls of their peeled lodgepole cabins. Due to the large amount of snow that fell in the forests, some Swedish builders constructed two roofs on their cabins: the first acted as a snow roof, while the second ensured a waterproof environment for the occupant below. Evidence of this work can still be seen in tie hack camps located in the Medicine Bow National Forest. The influence of Swedish immigrants was not limited to forested areas; ranchers and other settlers observed their skill and hired them to construct other types of buildings.

In his book *Ranch on the Laramie*, author Ted Olson recalls his youth in rural Wyoming and

Nicholas Swan Cabin, Sublette County.
The Swan homestead cabin is an example of folk architecture. Using cottonwood logs obtained locally, Nicholas Swan built the structure himself between 1878 and 1880. By the time this photo was taken, the original sod roof had been replaced.

Oxford Horse Barn, Albany County.
This huge log barn is approximately 150 feet long and was constructed in the nineteenth century. It is an example of piece-sur-piece construction.

remembers Swedish builder Ole Viklund:

"He was a hulking Swede, dark, dour, taciturn, whom Papa had hired to build a new bunkhouse. He had a reputation as a master log worker; he lost no time in demonstrating that it was well earned. Papa and Oscar were pretty good axmen, but Ole was an artist. It was a treat to watch him pare away the round of a big log, swinging the ax with effortless rhythm, until two sides were as flat and smooth as if they had gone through a planing mill. Then he would shape the other sides, notching one, hewing the obverse to a shallow V, so that one log would fit snugly into another, without need of chinking or plaster. You see log houses built that way in Scandinavian countries; if you find one in America you can safely assume that it was put up by a Swede or a Norwegian."

Traditional buildings constructed within a specific geographic region can also be considered folk. For example, in what appears to be an isolated enclave within the state, the plains south and west of Laramie contain several very unusual log barns. Although the ethnic origin of these buildings has not been verified, local tradition

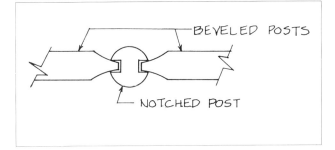

Above—Drawn piece-sur-piece detail.
This line drawing shows a birds-eye view of piece-sur-piece construction, the viewpoint is from the top of a vertical log looking down. *(Illustration by Jamie Wells.)*

Left—Photographic detail of piece-sur-piece construction.
This photograph illustrates how log walls sections are connected to produce a long log wall for a barn. In the United States piece-sur-piece construction is usually associated with military structures. In Wyoming, both military and agricultural structures were constructed with this method.

indicates that Swedish tie hacks built the "piece-sur-piece" barns for large horse ranches. The term refers to the manner in which the logs were stacked horizontally one on top of another and then inserted into vertical logs with a tenon. The vertical logs joining the horizontal logs occurred at fifteen to eighteen foot intervals. When the barns were raised between 1880 to 1910, the builders probably decided to use piece-sur-piece construction because shorter logs were easier to acquire and easier to handle. Also the piece-sur-piece construction method allowed longer walls to be constructed, creating a larger barn. Piece-sur-piece construction in the United States is normally associated with military construction, so the piece-sur-piece barns are relatively rare.

Wyoming's folk architecture is not limited to rural areas; some of the state's most interesting folk artifacts are located in cities and towns. Laramie's Scandinavian Lutheran Church, now known as the Landmark Pentecostal Church, exhibits its ethnic origins. Built in 1885, the church displays noteworthy Scandinavian characteristics such as a square steeple that projects out from the facade, an east-west orientation, a front door on the west side, and an interior altar facing east.

Folklorists and cultural geographers who analyze folk structures frequently refer to interior plans to help determine the origin of buildings. An interior plan reveals how the structure was actually used by its occupants. Unfortunately, this book is limited to the discussion of exterior features although interiors are important when discussing architecture.

The bedrock of Wyoming's architecture is its people—an independent people who carved dugouts into hills, cut trees and crafted them into sturdy log buildings, and joined together to build communities. Wyoming people built, lived in and preserved buildings which appealed to them and served their needs. Although architectural guides offer multitudes of methods and typologies which can used in historical interpretation, the "people" element remains the foundation when interpreting Wyoming's buildings.

Landmark United Pentecostal Church, Laramie, Albany County.
Originally known as the Scandinavian Lutheran Church, this religious structure is a good example of folk architecture. The church displays characteristics associated with the Scandinavians.

· WM · DUBOIS · ARCHITE[CT]
· CHEYENNE · WYOMIN[G]

Left—

Landmark Apartments, Cheyenne, Laramie County.

William Dubois designed the Landmark Apartments. To publicize his project, this sketch was printed on the front page of the Wyoming State Tribune on June 3, 1920. The article stated, "The general construction will be semi-fireproof and it will cost $210,000."
(Reproduction courtesy of the Wyoming State Tribune, Cheyenne.)

Wyoming Architects

Wyoming is graced with a number of noteworthy architect-designed buildings. Several of these buildings were designed by world-renowned architects whose offices were located outside the state of Wyoming. However, architects based in Wyoming also designed many structures of note.

Included among the out-of-state designers are nineteenth-century architects Henry Hobson Richardson and Henry Van Brunt who left architectural remnants in Wyoming to attest to their skill, including the Ames Monument and the Union Pacific Depot in Cheyenne. Robert Reamer designed one of the world's most outstanding log structures, Yellowstone Park's Old Faithful Inn, in 1902. The design firm of William and Arthur Fisher planned and executed construction of a very livable and attractive company town, now called Sinclair. Gilbert Stanley Underwood's firm

Architect William Dubois. William Dubois was one of Wyoming's most skilled and prolific architects. (Photo courtesy of Jean and George Dubois.)

completed a design for the Union Pacific railroad depot in Torrington. Even world-renown architect Frank Lloyd Wright designed a home near Cody during the 1950s. Lesser known architects came to Wyoming from nearby cities like Denver, Billings, and Salt Lake City to construct important buildings such as UW's Old Main (Frederick Albert Hale), the administration building at the State Penitentiary (Walter E. Ware) and numerous other structures throughout the state.

Equally important to students of Wyoming historic architecture are Wyoming-based architects such as Dubois, Garbutt and Weidner, Goodrich, Hitchcock, Julien, Krusmark, Porter, and Rainsford.

This book's purpose is not to offer a complete history of all of Wyoming's noted designers nor an exhaustive analysis of their work, but rather to provide a brief overview of a few representative architects with formal academic training who practiced in Wyoming. Some of these men received formal training in the field of architecture, while others were trained in engineering or associated disciplines. Many were founding members of the Wyoming Chapter of the American Institute of Architects chartered during the late 1940s.

Supreme Court and State Library Building, Cheyenne, Laramie County.
One of Dubois's most interesting governmental buildings is the Supreme Court/State Library Building. Dubois combined Neoclassical and Art Deco elements.

Cheyenne architect William Dubois was one of the most prolific and versatile of the Wyoming architects. Dubois came to Cheyenne to supervise the construction of the Carnegie Library and decided to stay. Educated at the Chicago School of Architecture during the late nineteenth century, Dubois was a proficient designer who utilized architectural styles ranging from Beaux Arts Classicism to Romanesque Revival to commercial styles popular at the turn of the century.

Governmental buildings throughout the state illustrate his versatility. The State of Wyoming hired Dubois to execute drawings for a variety of institutions including the east and west wings of the State Capitol. The list of substantial buildings Dubois designed is extensive; it includes Carnegie libraries, the Laramie and Albany County Courthouses, residential buildings, hotels, schools, commercial structures, and Masonic temples.

Two of the most distinctive commercial buildings in Cheyenne's historic downtown are Dubois designs—the Plains Hotel and the Hynds Building. Although the exterior of the Plains is a typical commercial design of the period, the interior ornamentation was a fascinating mixture of Native American and western motifs. Unfortunately,

58

Natrona County High School, Casper.
Arthur Garbutt and C.T. Weidner designed a highly ornate educational building. The terra cotta details illustrate that money was available for decorative details.

most of the original interior decor is now gone.

The Hynds Building is a white terra cotta clad edifice with highly decorative and unusual leaded glass windows above the storefront windows. Other Wyoming towns also have numerous Dubois designed buildings.

Arthur Garbutt, a structural engineer and graduate of Massachusetts Institute of Technology, and C. T. Weidner, his draftsman, practiced in Casper during the boom period in the early twentieth century. Expensive buildings adorned with rich terra cotta embellishments are hallmarks of Garbutt and Weidner. Typical of Garbutt and Weidner's work in Casper are substantial schools, fraternal organizations' buildings, and residential and commercial structures, among them Natrona County High School, the Townsend Hotel, Saint Anthony's Church, the Tripeny Building, and the Odd Fellows' and the Elks' Buildings. Garbutt and Weidner also designed the Teton Hotel in Riverton. In addition to his Wyoming practice, Garbutt taught architecture at Colorado Agriculture and Mining College.

Leon Goodrich began drawing buildings as a boy. After attending the University of Wyoming,

Natrona County High School, Casper.
Although Casper was experiencing an oil boom when NCHS was built, the decision to construct the building was extremely controversial. The building was elaborate for the time and was considered extravagant by some.

Goodrich worked with William Dubois in Cheyenne. In 1917, during an oil boom, Goodrich moved to Casper.

Goodrich's most noteworthy design was the Casper National Guard Armory that was demolished during the 1980s. Goodrich was one of the founding members of the Wyoming Chapter American Institute of Architects.

Goodrich sometimes collaborated with Casper architect Karl Krusmark. Krusmark came to Casper as an architect for Midwest Oil Company and designed what later became the Casper Women's Clubhouse. Goodrich and Krusmark, in collaboration, produced designs for numerous schools in Casper, Riverton, and Mills. Yet, their most noteworthy design is the Natrona County Courthouse with its distinctive frieze depicting county history and its unique western interior. Both men were involved in some of the earliest historic preservation projects in Wyoming at Forts Fetterman, Laramie, and Bridger.

Wilbur Hitchcock came to Wyoming in 1908 to escape South Dakota's pollen which aggravated his hay fever. After obtaining engineering degrees from both the University of Wyoming and the University of Colorado, Hitchcock became an assistant and associate professor in the Engineering Department at Wyoming's university. In 1921, Hitchcock opened an architectural office in Laramie and designed several buildings on the campus including structures now known as Aven Nelson and McWhinnie Halls and the Engineering Building. In association with William Dubois, a collaborative effort produced the Half Acre Gymnasium at the university and the Albany County Courthouse. Within the City of Laramie, Hitchcock designed the Ivinson Home for Women, Laramie High School (now the Laramie Civic Center), Nellie Isle and Whiting Schools and the Cooper Mansion. Double silos added to the university's livestock barn, originally Wyoming's Territorial Prison, were another example of Hitchcock's work.

According to his daughter Elinor Hitchcock Mullens, her father was fond of the Gothic motif. McWhinnie Hall and other Laramie buildings illustrate Hitchcock's skill when employing Gothic elements. Wilbur Hitchcock's architectural work was cut short by his untimely death in 1930, but his sons, Clinton and Eliot, continued in their father's footsteps and started an architectural practice in Laramie after World War II. The Hitchcock

McWhinnie Hall, University of Wyoming, Laramie, Albany County. Wilbur Hitchcock designed several buildings on the U.W. campus. Hitchcock's designs varied depending on the client's needs.

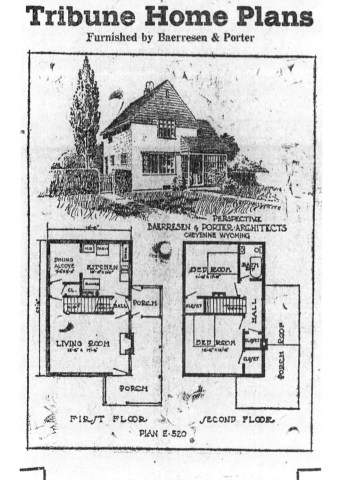

Tribune Home Plans

Furnished by Baerresen & Porter

PLAN E-520

Cheyenne architects Albert A. Baerresen and Frederick Hutchinson Porter used the Home Builders' page in the Wyoming State Tribune to advertise residential designs. The Home Builders' page was a regular Thursday feature in the newspaper during 1920. This ad, printed on July 8, 1920, stated: "It is designed in a domestic English type and appears so domestic and homey that one would instantly remark that here is not merely a house or dwelling, but a real home." (Advertisement courtesy of the Wyoming State Tribune, Cheyenne.)

brothers designed the Classroom Building on campus and worked as consultants during the restoration of the Capitol Building in Cheyenne.

J. P. Julien came to Wyoming as a veteran of the Civil War with a background in civil engineering. Julien was engaged in a variety of projects, perhaps the most macabre of which was designing gallows. He designed the gallows at the Wyoming State Penitentiary in Rawlins, and he also designed the Cheyenne gallows used to execute notorious outlaw Tom Horn. Additionally, Julien designed the Idleman House in Cheyenne, now Schrader's Funeral Home, and Cheyenne's red sandstone First Methodist Church.

Frederick Hutchinson Porter, known as "Bunk," was an architect committed to preserving Wyoming's historic buildings. He believed that the Union Pacific depot, the old post office and the Carnegie Library, all in Cheyenne, were irreplaceable, and he wrote editorials to encourage their preservation. Today, only the Union Pacific Depot remains.

Bunk Porter started private practice in Wyoming in 1920. He considered Cheyenne's First Presbyterian Church to be the "best job" he ever did. Buildings at the University of Wyoming such as the Agriculture Building as well as public structures such as the Carbon County Courthouse are typical of his approach to design. In addition to his architectural work, Porter was a skilled artist who painted watercolors and designed stage sets for local theater groups.

One of Wyoming's most eccentric architects was George Rainsford, occasionally referred to by locals as "Lord Rainsford." Rainsford had an unusual spiritual quest in which he reputedly asked God to prove His existence by striking Rainsford dead with a bolt of lightning. Lightning did not kill the architect.

Rainsford came to Wyoming from New York after the Civil War, trained as both a civil engineer and architect. Yet Rainsford spent a great deal of his family's money and his energy on breeding fine horses. His ranch, the Diamond, was headquartered outside of Chugwater where he designed an extensive complex of stone buildings, including masonry barns. Rainsford supposedly designed residences for friends and acquaintances. Several houses in Cheyenne's historic district named for the architect display Rainsford's talent for combining unusual roof shapes and angles. The architect was especially fond of combining elements from the Shingle and Queen Anne styles.

Other architects, equally skilled, but perhaps not as eccentric as Rainsford, lived and practiced in the state.

But the majority of Wyoming's historic buildings were not designed by academically-trained architects for specific sites, but rather were designed and constructed by carpenters and builders. Men such as Moses Patrick Keefe, who built the State Capitol, numerous churches and commercial buildings, as well as residences, played an important role. Some of Wyoming's historic builders, contractors, and carpenters left their names behind in listings in city directories and newspapers.

Still other skilled traditional designers and builders do not have their names recorded in any historical documents. Unnamed loggers and tie hacks are responsible for some of Wyoming's most interesting structures.

Wyoming's architectural diversity is based on the famous and the unknown, the schooled and the "naturals," the tie hacks and the university professors. Each made integral contributions.

Left—Main Street, Hartville, Platte County.
A community with interesting architecture in the "community development" theme, Hartville dates from 1884 and is said to be the oldest incorporated town in Wyoming. The copper mines played out in about 1887, but iron ore was discovered nearby soon after. Most of the false fronts were constructed in the 1900-1907 period when the population was at its peak of about 750 residents.

Historic Themes

Wyoming's architecture can be grouped into general thematic categories such as agriculture, community development, military architecture and so on. These categories are based on historic themes that influenced the settlement and development of the state. Within each theme are examples of architect-designed, manufactured and folk architecture.

AGRICULTURE Wyoming's ranches and farms contain some of the state's most interesting architecture. Economically, Wyoming's agriculture has seen a range of extremes—from the hand-to-mouth survival of homesteaders living in dugouts to the courtly lifestyle of British "cattle barons"—with many levels in between. This has created widely varied architectural resources. As a preservationist, I always arrive at a ranch or farm with a sense of expectancy—a sense that

Mormon Barn, Grand Teton National Park, Teton County.
This log barn with its majestic backdrop is a familiar site to people in Wyoming. The barn was constructed by Mormon settlers during the early twentieth century in an area known as Mormon Row. The area was eventually incorporated into Grand Teton National Park.

there may be a barn, homestead cabin, or residence unlike any other structure in the state.

People who drive through Wyoming on an interstate highway miss the most compelling part of historic preservation in a under-populated state like Wyoming—historic buildings in their natural surroundings. Whether one looks at a dryland farm surrounded by rocky outcroppings in southeastern Wyoming or surveys a ranch with incredible vistas along the Green River in Sublette County, few historic experiences compare.

To describe ranch architecture in terms of utility or function ignores the craftsmanship that is exhibited in many of the log or stone ranch buildings. A ranch or farm needs to be viewed as a cultural landscape. Instead of separating components—the corrals from the outbuildings, the house from the use of the fields, the irrigation ditches from the barn—the land needs to be viewed as an architectural whole. It is the integration of the natural landscape with historic buildings that make some of Wyoming's historic ranches truly unique. Carbon County's Stone Wall Ranch is only one example of this phenomenon.

Ranches and farms with interesting folk structures abound. Although a few agricultural buildings, such as those at the Diamond Ranch built by George Rainsford, were architect-designed, many of Wyoming's ranches were constructed either by their owners or by local craftsmen. After the turn of the century and especially by 1920, the impact of technology affected the type of buildings that were constructed on farms and ranches. Sears and Roebuck as well as Montgomery Ward sold barns through their catalogs, while the University of Wyoming's Extension Service distributed plans and detailed information on how to construct efficient agricultural buildings. Ranch houses, such as bungalows and foursquares, were also purchased through the Sears catalogs. One finds buildings on Wyoming's ranches that fit into all three broad architectural categories.

Wyoming ranches and farms were not built around a standard formula or typical layout. Generally, farms and ranches within the United States followed a European farmstead model of detached buildings grouped around a yard. Architecturally, the determining factors included

Valley Ranch, Park County.
This modest log cabin, located at the Valley Ranch, is typical of many of Wyoming's earliest cabins. The builder used materials, logs and sod, that could be obtained in the area. (Drawing by Jamie Wells.)

the settler's ethnic background, topography, availability of water, and the individual needs of the agricultural unit. The buildings that a rancher or farmer needed depended on the types of crops and livestock he raised, his location, his irrigation needs, and the lay of the land.

Agricultural buildings vary within regions of Wyoming. Substantial stone houses and barns were constructed in Sheridan and Johnson Counties along Piney Creek. The log piece-sur-piece barns and out buildings of the Laramie Plains are rather unusual. The ethnic background of the builder and the availability of materials were strong determinants in the type of buildings that were constructed.

The history of Wyoming ranching and farming is complicated by the numerous changes in legislation over the years. Stockraising began in Wyoming long before the area became a territory, much less a state. The availability of inexpensive grazing land was an incentive to both Americans and foreigners to settle in the state. People established themselves along drainages where water was available. Ranchers used land that was in the public domain, actually owning little of the property that their livestock grazed.

Part of the architectural legacy of the open-range period is a wide variety of "cattle baron" mansions in cities and substantial barns found on ranches. Not all of the early ranchers during the 1870s and 1880s were wealthy, but the wealthy did establish some notable buildings. The piece-sur-piece edifices paid for by the British on the Laramie Plains ranches and the Gothic Revival house established by the Scottish owners at the Swan Land and Cattle Company in Chugwater were substantial investments. Early homesteaders, such as Nicholas Swan in Sublette County, did not have the financial means to construct large houses and outbuildings. Swan's log cabin [see Chapter Three] is also representative of the early cattle industry. Many of the earliest ranchers survived by using locally available construction materials to build what was required.

Where logs were unavailable or the settler's funds were limited, newcomers constructed dugouts in the sides of hills. In a way, dugouts are self explanatory; the builder literally dug out the side of a hill and fabricated a roof and door. The residents, hearing stories of cows falling through roofs and snakes inviting themselves inside, hoped their personal experiences would not prove too offensive. Dugouts were usually considered temporary shelter until something more permanent could be constructed.

As is typical of the economic cycles that seem to plague the West, the first "bust" in the Wyoming cattle industry occurred in the 1880s due to weather conditions, overgrazing, cattle diseases, management problems, and market factors. Yet, the failure of the huge cattle operations in the 1880s made available more land for the smaller agricultural operator.

The years 1890-1920 brought great changes to the landscape of Wyoming. Barbed wire fenced grazing land into units, and smaller herds of cattle occupied pastures. Ranchers put up hay and alfalfa for supplemental winter livestock feed, instead of "wintering" cattle on only the forage provided by the range. Although sheep had been raised in Wyoming since the state's earliest days, sheep became a significant part of the agricultural economy. The conflicts that occurred between sheep and cattle raisers during this period still provide material for heated debate.

Left—Dryland Farm, Niobrara County.
Many settlers came to Wyoming to take advantage of free agricultural land. Thousands attempted dryland farming, but most did not succeed due to Wyoming's low annual rainfall. The abandoned buildings are all that remain of many of these dryland dreams.

Right—Hansen Barns, Teton County.
The log and frame barns at Clifford Hansen's ranch in Teton County have the appearance of Danish barns with horizontal logs on the bottom portions and vertical framing on the tops.

LX Bar Ranch, Chicken House, Campbell County. This stone chicken house could be Wyoming's most elegant chicken coop. The stone buildings on the LX Bar were constructed by Scandinavian stone masons for John B. Kendrick.

The Wyoming Experiment Station's Bulletin Number 38 published in 1898 said, "The typical Wyoming ranch is everywhere thought of as a collection of low buildings, fences and hay stacks, without a tree in sight…. This condition is rapidly changing however. With the development of the irrigated farm these temporary ranches are being transformed into comfortable homes." The Experiment Station strongly encouraged farmers and ranchers to plant trees and ornamental shrubs.

The railroads, the University of Wyoming's Experiment Station, Wyoming state government, and private enterprise recruited substantial numbers of homesteaders to Wyoming by spreading the popular idea of dryland farming. The concept behind dryland farming in arid and semiarid regions of Wyoming entailed trapping and conserving natural rainfall within the soil to make an area more productive. Supposedly, irrigation was unnecessary for successful dryland farming. Over 80,000 homestead entries were filed between 1910 and 1934, but less than half of the homesteaders were granted a final patent. Many others sold out and moved on, relinquishing ownership.

Left—LX Bar Ranch, kitchen and bunkhouse, Campbell County. The LX Bar buildings, built in the early twentieth century, are unusual for a Wyoming ranch. The stone masons lived at the ranch site and constructed the kitchen with the diamond-shaped window, the bunkhouse in the foreground, as well as barns, the ranch house, and even the outbuildings.

Below—LX Bar Ranch, stone barns, Campbell County. The unusually shaped stone barns were constructed for use by both horses and cattle.

The landscape of north, east and central Wyoming is littered with the remnants of failed dryland farms. Although the homestead concept may have been unrealistic from the outset for Wyoming's arid lands , the drought of the twenties and thirties and the Depression hastened the demise of many dryland farms. Often a leaning windmill tower and the skeleton of a small frame abode are all that remain to mark the site of the dreams of a dryland homesteader.

Some farmers and ranchers enlarged their holdings during the early twentieth century.

Manville Kendrick had stone masons construct impressive sandstone ranch buildings in northeast Wyoming. As manufactured materials became more readily available because of improved transportation, farmers and ranchers were less likely to gather and process their own construction materials.

Rural electrification and gasoline-powered tractors accelerated changes to the rural landscape. Extension agents suggested methods to make farms and ranches more sanitary and efficient. The agents even provided interior decorating tips. Yet depressed farm prices and the continuing drought through the thirties made agriculture a risky occupation in the state.

This brief history of agriculture is needed to explain the current appearance of Wyoming ranches. As ranches and farms failed, the buildings located at an unsuccessful place were frequently moved to another more successful locale. Over the years, ranches became conglomerations of previous farms and ranches. Numerous Wyoming ranches have a rather interesting grouping of log buildings, frame buildings, a stone building or two, a dilapidated dugout, a steel pole barn and a modular home. It is an extraordinary ranch that does not have buildings that were brought in from somewhere else.

In fact, some of Wyoming's most economically successful ranches and farms no longer illustrate their historic origins. As in other places, historic buildings were replaced when they were no longer considered useful.

Wyoming farms and ranches contain a variety of building types that include barns, ranch houses, bunkhouses, homesteaders' cabins, cookhouses, outbuildings, corrals, fences, stockpens, stock watering facilities, tankhouses, and truck loading gates.

COMMUNITY DEVELOPMENT/ COMMERCIAL ARCHITECTURE

Wyoming's community development architecture is harder to define in specific terms than other themes. Community development pertains to the actual growth and development of an urban area, especially the commercial core. It also relates to the maturation of a community and the introduction of culture, both through the stage and with other cultural amenities. Here, the

Livestock Exhibit and Sale Pavilion, Sheridan County.
This substantial stone building is a rather elegant part of both Wyoming's agricultural and commercial architecture.

words community development and commercial architecture are used in reference to Wyoming's buildings such as hotels, schools, theaters, libraries, stores, service clubs, banks, livery stables, saloons, and restaurants.

The commercial section was the heartbeat of a town; during the nineteenth century a town's economic success depended on the viability of the commercial core. Some towns had the economic advantage of being a county seat while other municipalities survived because of their role in state government. For example, the state penitentiary in Rawlins and the university in Laramie played key roles in those towns' growth.

Traditionally in the eastern United States, towns and villages grew along rivers or streams; in Wyoming, too, many municipalities had their start along waterways. However for transportation purposes, the railroad was much more important to the development of Wyoming than waterways. Therefore, a town's oldest buildings are frequently found close to the railroad tracks.

The arrival of the railroad created substantial urban growth. This was particularly true as the Union Pacific completed its route across southern

First Security Bank, Rock Springs, Sweetwater County.
This bank is one of the most significant buildings in southwest Wyoming. The terra cotta clad exterior with extensive terra cotta decoration is unusual for that part of the state. The bank directors wanted to project an appearance of stability and permanence.

Wyoming in the 1860s. The state's Union Pacific towns were platted by the Chief Engineer for the company, Grenville Dodge. Many Wyoming towns were platted according to a standard grid with rectangular blocks, straight streets, and right-angle intersections, a strategy which had proven successful in the Midwest.

The earliest Wyoming towns were generally service areas for stockraisers and farmers; eventually energy development also became a stimulus for the growth of towns. In comparison to other states, Wyoming still has an amazingly small number of incorporated towns and cities because of the state's small, wide-spread population.

Wyoming's community development architecture has a rich variety which illustrate all three types of architecture: architect-designed, manufactured, and folk.

The first buildings in a commercial area were normally of frame or log construction. Some buildings may have been tents while others were false front construction with large parapet walls that dominated the front of the stores. As a town prospered, the boom town architecture was replaced with more substantial masonry buildings,

Fox Theatre, Rawlins, Carbon County.
The Fox Theatre in Rawlins was at one time both a live performance theatre and a movie house. The terra cotta ornamentation on the upper story is a rather fanciful display to attract attention to the building. The first story has been altered.

Buffalo Bar, Buffalo, Johnson County.
This bar has an intact sheet metal storefront, also known as an iron front, manufactured by George Mesker of Evansville, Indiana. The storefront was probably selected from a catalog and shipped to Buffalo by rail.

usually of brick or stone. A few cities such as Lander and Rock Springs have an occasional frame false front building remaining in their downtown area.

Architectural elements purchased through catalogs and delivered by rail adorned many of the commercial buildings constructed in the 1880s, the 1890s and early twentieth century. Entire sheet metal storefronts with cornices, pilasters, lintels, windows and doors could be purchased from manufacturers in the Midwest and Rocky Mountain regions. These storefronts are referred to as iron fronts or stamped metal fronts. Some manufacturers offered design advice for merchants and would calculate exactly what was needed for construction and then design a facade for a specific lot.

In Wyoming, one frequently finds commercial facades adorned by sheet metal fronts that were manufactured by Mesker Brothers of St. Louis, Missouri, or George Mesker of Evansville, Indiana. The Buffalo Bar in Buffalo, Wyoming, is an excellent example of a George Mesker sheet metal front with pilasters, threshold and ornamentation all shipped to Buffalo for this structure. The sheet

Left—General Store, Aladdin, Crook County.

Right—County Library, Buffalo, Johnson County.

These two buildings have both served their community well, although their architecture varies greatly.

The Aladdin store, at left, was constructed in 1890 and was the heart of the commercial area. It is almost all that remains of Aladdin.

The Johnson County Library, at right, is a lasting legacy to Buffalo funded by Andrew Carnegie, the Pittsburgh steel magnate. W.H. Butler completed the design for the Neoclassical library in 1909. Several Carnegie libraries remain in Wyoming.

Right—Standard School, Keeline, Niobrara County. School buildings were often the social hub of the community as well as the educational center. This school at Keeline is an example of a "standard-ized" rural school. In 1918, the State of Wyoming established guidelines for the construction of rural schools in an effort to promote better hygiene and lighting.

Left—Community Hall, Cowley, Big Horn County. A few communities built community halls which were separate from schools. The Civilian Conservation Corps constructed the Cowley Community Hall during the depression of the 1930s. It was used as both a community gathering place and a gymnasium.

Elks' Club Building, Casper, Natrona County.
Designed by Garbutt and Weidner, this building indicates the importance of the Elks to Casper. This fraternal organization obviously could afford a substantial and ornate building during one of Casper's boom periods.

metal or iron front facades are prime examples of manufactured architecture, and most of Wyoming's commercial areas have several. The buildings themselves reflect the accepted architectural styles of the day and demonstrate what materials were shipped from other locales to Wyoming.

After the turn of the century, architectural tastes changed, and more terra cotta was used in prominent Wyoming buildings such as the Casper Elks' Club, the Natrona County High School, and the Hynds Building in Cheyenne. The twentieth-century architecture of Casper illustrates its growth during the teens and the twenties due to the oil boom. Terra cotta became available to architects or builders through catalogs. Decorative terra cotta ornamentation in a variety of colors adorned commercial facades in larger Wyoming cities.

While Casper's architecture reveals the influence of the oil boom, many of Wyoming's towns also illustrate the bust of the thirties. Substantially fewer buildings were constructed in commercial areas during the early thirties; those that were built were less decorative than earlier structures.

Cady Building, Sheridan, Sheridan County.
Once an opera house, this building was carefully restored in the 1980s. The building's elaborate stone ornamental features make it one of Sheridan's most interesting commercial structures. (Drawing by Jamie Wells)

Smith-Sherlock Store, South Pass City, Fremont County
This commercial building in the mining town of South Pass City is a good example of "boom town" architecture with its false front. As an example of folk architecture, the building is a lasting reminder of the gold mining heyday.

The materials used in community development architecture vary somewhat according to locale. For instance, more stone buildings appear in Cody's downtown than in other towns. Evanston has a great variety of sheet metal fronts, while Casper has more terra cotta buildings than any other municipality in the state.

Commercial buildings, as well as other historic buildings, physically illustrate a town's history. Although the first story of many commercial structures has been changed, frequently the upper stories remain unaltered and serve as good descriptive elements in the town's history.

Yet, commercial buildings only tell part of the story in reference to a community's evolution. Other community buildings also reveal pertinent information about development and history. Andrew Carnegie and his largess helped to establish dozens of Carnegie libraries throughout the state. Although local or county governments agreed to maintain the buildings, Carnegie actually paid for the structures themselves. Of the few remaining Carnegie libraries left in the state, most reveal Neoclassical elements. The library, as well as occasional opera houses or theaters, was crucial to

the social and cultural life of a town. Later, movie theaters were found in larger urban areas, and also, somewhat surprisingly, in many small towns such as Baggs, Cokeville, and Jay Em.

Wyoming's variety of commercial and community buildings offer architectural insight into the history of its communities.

GOVERNMENT BUILDINGS   Some of the state's most prominent structures are associated with federal, state or local governments.

Although a few buildings have vernacular origins, the vast majority of governmental buildings were designed by an architect for a specific location. Most of Wyoming's earliest territorial governmental buildings did not survive; therefore, the majority of the state's historic governmental structures date from the 1880s to the 1930s.

Western historians have chronicled the crucial role the federal government played and continues to play in the survival of the West. Water

Far left—Territorial Penitentiary, Laramie, Albany County.
Recently this nineteenth-century territorial penitentiary, originally constructed in stages from 1872 to 1889, was transformed from a sheep barn to a museum because of interest among the people of Laramie. The building is one of the few governmental structures remaining in Wyoming from territorial days.

Left—Administration Building, Historic State Penitentiary, Rawlins, Carbon County.
The massive Administration Building constructed during the 1890s is Romanesque Revival in style. The barred windows and doors give the building a foreboding appearance. Utilized as a prison until 1980, the complex is now a historic district listed on the National Register of Historic Places.

Post Office, Thermopolis, Hot Springs County.
Before this building was completed in 1933 at the cost of approximately $90,000, citizens tried to persuade the federal government that locally quarried stone should be used in their post office. Their efforts failed and limestone was imported from Indiana. The design and execution make the Thermopolis Post Office one of Wyoming's outstanding federal buildings. *(Drawing by Jamie Wells.)*

Below—Federal Courthouse and Post Office, Lander, Fremont County. The Office of Supervising Architect of the Treasury was responsible for the design of this ornate federal building completed in 1912. The Supervising Architect, James Knox Taylor, believed federal buildings should be both beautiful and representative of the ideals of democracy. During the early twentieth century, Wyoming received elaborate post offices due largely to the work of Senator F.E. Warren, a member of the Senate Committee on Public Buildings and Grounds.

Above—Post Office, Basin, Big Horn County. Even small communities benefitted from the federal government's largess. The Basin Post Office was finished in 1919.

Left—Town Hall, Lost Springs, Converse County.
With a population of nine, Lost Springs has a less pretentious-looking town hall. Built in 1914, the town hall is a false front building.

Right—City Hall, Rock Springs, Sweetwater County.
Architect Martin Didicus Kern of Salt Lake City designed the Romanesque Revival city hall for Rock Springs in 1894. After functioning as a governmental building for years, the building became a museum during the 1980s.
(Drawing by Herbert E. Dawson.)

development projects, military establishments, and other sources of federal assistance are an integral part of life for most Wyoming residents. Many of the state's most significant historic buildings such as Old Faithful Inn, located in Yellowstone National Park, are administered by federal agencies. The federal government's role is not limited to parks or military associations but is represented in the vast array of federal agencies that operate within the state.

Federal buildings such as post offices are highly visible in most of Wyoming's downtowns. Especially in smaller urban areas, the design of the post office, which is frequently Neoclassical, may be unlike any other building in town. Normally, federal agencies employed their own architects who designed buildings, but some agencies hired contractual architects. For example, the Supervising Architect of the U.S. Treasury was responsible for designing many of the state's federal courthouses and post offices that were built from 1900 to 1930.

Generally, it was the practice of state and local governments to call for bids and request drawings when constructing major public buildings.

Veterans' Administration Medical Center, Cheyenne, Laramie County.
Constructed in stages, the main hospital building at the V.A. Center was first occupied in 1932. A Spanish Colonial motif with tile roofs gives the complex an attractive appearance.

During territorial days, architects from Denver and Salt Lake City were hired by state and local governments, but as Wyoming became more prosperous, architects moved to the state and bid competitively on governmental buildings. William Dubois of Cheyenne was a prolific architect who designed additions to the State Capitol, buildings at the State Penitentiary complex in Rawlins, and the Supreme Court Building in Cheyenne.

Not all the local government buildings were architect-designed. Several small communities still use buildings that had multiple uses and were probably built by someone in the community. Folk structures such as the town hall in Lost Springs, Wyoming, and the post office in Aladdin are a nice change from the Neoclassical facade of most governmental buildings.

Wyoming State Capitol Building, Cheyenne, Laramie County.
Designed by Toledo, Ohio, architect, David Gibbs, the building was completed in March 1888. Construction on the wings occurred in stages as the need for more room became apparent. Renovation of the Capitol took place during the 1970s.
(Photo by Mark Junge and Richard Collier.)

Coal Tipple, Reliance, Sweetwater County.
Local efforts in Sweetwater County ensured the preservation of this metallic coal tipple at Reliance. Men, women, and children worked inside the tipple sorting coal.

Industrial and Energy Development

Wyoming's historic architecture is linked to energy development, not only because of the actual facilities that were built as a direct result of mineral extraction or oil refining, but also due to the prosperity that energy development triggered in the state. The Salt Creek Oil Field, north of Casper, brought architectural diversity to that city in the form of substantial buildings highly ornamented with terra cotta. The economy of Rock Springs, Hanna, Kemmerer and other towns were dependent on coal mines. It is a familiar story heard throughout Wyoming and the West.

Most of Wyoming's industrial and energy-related buildings can be called functional; aesthetics were not considered. Yet the noteworthy exception is the entire town of Parco, later renamed Sinclair. The well-known architectural firm of Fisher and Fisher from Denver was hired in the twenties by Producers and Refiners Corporation, PARCO, to design the public, commercial and

Parco Inn, Sinclair, Carbon County.
The town of Sinclair was planned as a model company town for 1500 people. It is Wyoming's most interesting, as well as most elegant company town. Architects William and Arthur Fisher of Denver designed public buildings, an inn, a theatre, a church, and housing for supervisors and workers, all in a Spanish Colonial motif.

These two Carbon County photos illustrate the tie between energy development and architecture in Wyoming.

Left—Sinclair Refinery, Sinclair, Carbon County.
The PARCO refinery began operating during the early 1920s. In 1943, the property was acquired by Sinclair. The refinery still operates today.
(Photo by Mark Junge.)

Right— Street scene, McFadden, Carbon County.
McFadden is a typical oil company town with frame houses and public buildings.

Right—Piedmont Charcoal Kilns, Uinta County.
A different type of industrial architecture, these beautiful charcoal kilns were built around 1869. They were used by early settlers to transform wood into charcoal.

Right—Grain Silo, Clearmont, Sheridan County.
Sometimes called "mountains of the plains," grain silos are an important part of the landscape in an agricultural area.

residential buildings for the town. Company towns are common, yet Fisher and Fisher designed a town unlike any other in Wyoming.

The motif for Parco's architecture was Spanish Colonial. Tile roofs, stucco exteriors, and iron balconies gave the town a Spanish feel. The architects integrated a plaza into the plan and incorporated Spanish concepts into traffic patterns and street intersections.

The Parco Inn, constructed at substantial cost to the oil company, is the architectural highlight of the town. The housing for the corporate officers, and even the workers' housing, is also noteworthy. Not all of the buildings were individually designed. William Fisher, as president of the mountain division of the Architect's Small House Service Bureau, was familiar with the concept of manufactured housing. He had designed some smaller and less expensive homes for the bureau's use, and several of these house designs were incorporated into the master plan for Parco.

In 1934, the name of the town was changed from Parco to Sinclair when Sinclair Oil Company acquired the refineries and the town.

Western Sugar Company Office, Lovell, Big Horn County.
The brick office with a tile roof contrasts with the surrounding industrial architecture of the sugar beet plant.

Wyoming's industrial architecture varies from the functional or manufactured-type, such as the Clearmont grain silo, to the architect-designed buildings of Sinclair (Parco) to the extraordinary craftsmanship exhibited in the masonry charcoal kilns. This variety illustrates the diverse nature of the state's industrial heritage.

MILITARY ARCHITECTURE

Wyoming's forts were built throughout the nineteenth century in response to the needs of early travelers. The United States Army's responsibility was to protect emigrants, and the Army accomplished its task by building numerous forts either along or near transportation corridors. Some of the emigrants used trails such as the Oregon or Bozeman Trails that crisscrossed the state, while others traveled by rail on the Union Pacific's transcontinental railroad after its completion.

The oldest fort in the state is Fort Laramie. Although the fort was initially a trading post, it became a military installation in 1849 with the mission to protect emigrants along the Oregon Trail. The Army constructed numerous other

Old Bedlam, Fort Laramie, Goshen County.

Old Bedlam, constructed as officers' quarters in 1849, is probably the oldest military building in the state. After the fort was abandoned in 1890, many of the buildings disappeared. Over the years, Old Bedlam lost its wings and part of the porch. The National Park Service acquired the site in 1938.

Three photographs of F. E. Warren Air Force Base, Cheyenne, Laramie County.

Left—Administration Building.

The 1894 Administration Building is now used as the base museum. The base received the prestigious National Trust Honor Award in 1991 for its outstanding historic preservation efforts.

Above—Horsehead Keystone, Veterinary Hospital.

The veterinary hospital, a necessary fixture for a cavalry camp, has an unusual horsehead keystone used to identify the building.

Right—Officers' Quarters.

Construction of many of the barracks and officers' quarters at Fort D. A. Russell, renamed F.E. Warren in 1930, occurred in the early twentieth century. The historic district at the base, with its tree-lined streets and hundreds of historic buildings and parade grounds, has the look and feel of an old cavalry base.

U. S. Engineer's Office, Yellowstone National Park.
The U.S. Engineer's Office at Fort Yellowstone was designed by the Minnesota architectural firm of Reed and Stem in 1903. The building is known locally as the "Pagoda" because of the Oriental influence in the design.

forts in Wyoming during the second half of the nineteenth century. Some of these forts, such as Fort D. A. Russell, were manned to assist in the protection of rail lines while others, such as Fort Fetterman, were constructed in response to conflicts with Native Americans.

The Army built Fort Yellowstone in 1886 to protect the nation's first national park, Yellowstone. In 1871, Camp Brown (originally Camp Augur) was moved northwest and renamed Fort Washakie with the mission of serving the Native Americans on the Wind River Reservation. The military had a role in twentieth-century Wyoming when prisoner of war camps were constructed near Powell and Douglas during World War II.

Although some of the buildings at Wyoming's forts were architect-designed for specific locations, the vast majority of the buildings were manufactured. Various Army or government offices rendered standardized plans for buildings at forts which account for the sameness among the structures. For example, plans for many of the buildings at Fort D. A. Russell (renamed F. E. Warren in the twentieth century) were obtained from the Office of the Quartermaster General.

Some of the first military buildings were most likely designed right at the building spot, in the folk tradition, using what resources the builders had on hand.

Generally, military buildings reflect several significant characteristics: the accepted architectural fashion of the time, the ever-important necessity of keeping building costs to a minimum, and the concern for a standardized approach to procurement and construction specifications.

The buildings at F. E. Warren Air Force Base in Cheyenne were built by architects who were well aware of the architectural fashions of the time. Within the United States during the late nineteenth century, applied ornamentation and unusual angles were the rage. Houses in the residential historic districts of Cheyenne reflect the social acceptance of using elaborate ornamental details. Yet, the buildings at Warren, even the Victorian buildings, tend to have fewer ornamental details than other buildings constructed during the 1880s and 1890s. The Warren buildings tend to be less complex in terms of their massing; for example, the roof lines are simpler.

Anna Miller Museum, Newcastle, Weston County.
This unusual stone false front building was originally associated with the National Guard in the Weston County area. Most recently, it has housed the Anna Miller Historical Museum.

Fort Fetterman, Converse County.
Established as a military post in 1867, at the junction of the Oregon and Bozeman Trails, Fort Fetterman played an important role in the Indian wars of the 1870s. The log officers' quarters is piece-sur-piece construction. This type of construction character-ized some military posts in the Rocky Mountain region. *(Photo by Liz Stambaugh.)*

Generally, the military used materials that were locally available. Many of the forts contain red brick buildings that were constructed with brick that was purchased nearby. The buildings at Fort Fetterman and Fort Sanders were primar-ily constructed from logs that were cut within close proximity to the fort.

Wyoming's historic military sites have a plethora of buildings types. Many of the mili-tary installations were communities unto them-selves and, therefore, had all the necessary support facilities. Residential structures include officers' quarters, non-commissioned officers' housing and enlisted men's barracks. Functional buildings such as barns and veterinary hospi-tals, guard houses, stores, jails, offices, adminis-tration buildings, warehouses, and hospitals are found at many of the extant military posts.

The grounds of the Veteran Administration Hospitals in Cheyenne and Sheridan also con-tain many historic structures.

RAILROAD When the United States Congress enacted legislation that enticed railroad entrepreneurs, the government, in its own way, ensured the growth and development of the area that would eventually become Wyoming. The construction of the first transcontinental railroad is closely linked with the actual settlement of permanent towns within the state.

Construction of the Union Pacific line in Wyoming began during 1867 and made a path along the southern corridor during the following year. Towns such as Cheyenne, Laramie, Rawlins, Green River, Rock Springs, and Evanston grew along with the railroad as Union Pacific representatives platted Wyoming's earliest settlements. With the railroad came rail buildings: depots, hotels, roundhouses, and other railroad structures.

Although Union Pacific's southern route dominated the rail business in the earliest years of Wyoming's settlement, by the turn of the century construction of rail lines through the central

Sheridan Inn, Sheridan County.
A joint effort of the Burlington and Missouri Railroad and the Sheridan Land Company financed the inn's construction. Thomas Kimball, an Omaha architect, designed the structure with its gabled dormers and huge veranda. Now a National Historic Landmark, the inn opened in 1893.

Union Pacific Roundhouse, Evanston, Uinta County.
This roundhouse, constructed around 1912, is Wyoming's last intact roundhouse. It is part of a larger complex of railroad maintenance buildings.

part of the state had established rail connections with Sheridan and Newcastle in the north and Casper and Douglas in the central part of the state. Ultimately by the end of World War I, vast areas in the Big Horn Basin and the central part of the state had been settled in large part due to the construction of the Burlington lines and the Chicago and Northwestern links.

In most Wyoming cities and towns, the railroad depot and associated rail structures were significant buildings that articulated the railroad's importance within the town. In the late nineteenth and early twentieth centuries, rail was a basic means of transportation, and the size and design of the depot easily demonstrated the railroad's importance. The depot was a focal point for the community and immediately conveyed the settlement's economic and social status.

As previously detailed, the Union Pacific's depot in Cheyenne is one of the most outstanding historic buildings in the Rocky Mountain West because of its Romanesque Revival design. The depot's roughcut stone work seems to blend in with, if not emulate, its surroundings. The building still has a great deal of integrity because,

Union Pacific Turntable, Evanston, Uinta County.
The turntable, supposedly still in working order, is one of a few turntables left in the state. Cars were moved via the table to different stalls in the roundhouse.

even though additions were made over the years, Union Pacific has worked to retain the original architectural style of the structure.

Some of Wyoming's railroad depots were designed by architects for specific locations, such as Cheyenne's. Thomas Kimball of Omaha designed the Sheridan Inn for the Chicago, Burlington, and Quincy Railroad. Other railroad buildings were designed by architectural firms which had contracts with the railroad company or by architects who were actually employees of the corporation. Therefore, most of the railroad buildings within the state fall into the tradition of architect-designed or manufactured architecture.

Standardized plans were used for depots throughout the midwest, especially for frame buildings. The Chief Engineer's Office for the Union Pacific was responsible for designing the depots in Rawlins, Laramie, and Evanston. None of the railroad depots seem to fall into the category of folk architecture.

Generally, the more substantial depots and associated rail buildings were made of brick. Many of the buildings, such as the roundhouse, machine shop, and storehouse in the Union Pacific complex in Evanston, were constructed of red brick.

Often smaller depots, such as the Union Pacific depot in Medicine Bow or the Chicago and Northwestern depot in Powder River, were made of wood.

The depots and associated structures reflect the architectural fashion or styles of the times. Cheyenne's depot expressed Union Pacific President Charles Adams's desire to build a substantial edifice. Wyoming's depots seem to be of a somewhat uniform appearance, whether brick or frame. Generally, the depots are one story, although there are exceptions such as the depots in Sheridan, Casper and Green River. Many sit low to the ground and have prominent entries to focus attention on the main door. The roofs generally are hipped, and large overhanging eaves often adorn the buildings.

Yet, depots are not the only type of rail structure found in Wyoming. Numerous ancillary buildings served the locomotives and tracks themselves. Entire complexes occupied important economic roles in the community. Few intact historic railroad complexes remain. The most

South Torrington U.P. Depot/ Homesteaders' Museum, Goshen County.
The noted architectural firm of Gilbert Stanley Underwood designed the South Torrington depot. The design for the 1926 depot is unique in the state.

outstanding example of a rail complex with a roundhouse that is still in use is the Evanston Union Pacific complex, although it is now used by an occupant other than the railroad.

Other types of rail structures in Wyoming complexes are engine houses, freight houses, power houses, snowsheds, relay stations, control towers, coal chutes and tipples, turntables, and water towers. In the early days of the railroad, the company frequently paid for the construction of a hotel located close to the depot. Although the original rail hotels are all but lost, significant examples do remain such as the Sheridan Inn.

Below—Union Pacific Depot, Medicine Bow, Carbon County.
This depot is a typical rural railroad station with huge brackets supporting overhanging eaves. The building now houses a local museum.

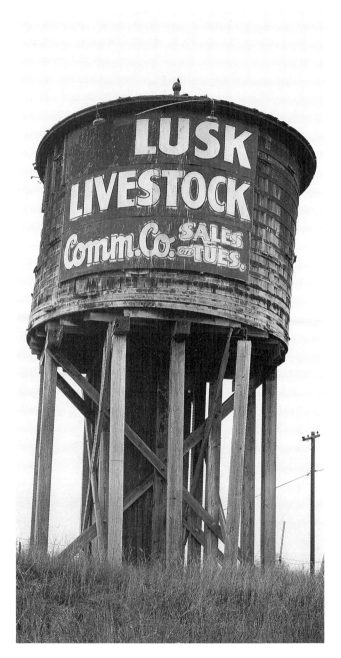

Left—Water Tower, Lusk, Niobrara County.
This wooden water tower that originally serviced steam engines is no longer located close to the depot. The tower is the last remaining wooden railroad tower in the state. *(Photo by Mark Junge.)*

Below—Burlington Northern Depot, Casper, Natrona County. Although no longer used by the railroad, the formidable Casper depot is a significant building located near the downtown area.

Medicine Wheel, Big Horn County.
This medicine wheel, located at the top of a mountain overlooking the Big Horn Basin, is part of a continuing religious tradition for Native Americans. In native cultures, religious sites are not necessarily architectural in form but are frequently natural sites.

RELIGIOUS Wyoming's religious architecture begins in prehistoric times. Some of the earliest designed and constructed structures found in Wyoming are the medicine wheel and the sun dance lodges built by Native Americans for religious purposes. In Native cultures, religious sites are not necessarily architectural in form, but are frequently natural sites with precisely arranged materials. A medicine wheel located on a mountain in the Big Horn Mountains is a sacred site for Native American tribes who continue to hold religious services there. Tribes also constructed sweat lodges and sun dance lodges from natural materials for their religious ceremonies as part of a continuing folk tradition.

As soon as the railroad reached Wyoming, people began erecting churches. To many, churches symbolized permanence, stability and spiritual well-being. Additionally churches served social needs; many religious structures served as local meeting places during territorial days. On some occasions, church buildings were

Right —Good Shepherd Church, Sundance, Crook County.
Gothic Revival elements are evident in the Good Shepherd Church of Sundance.
(Drawing by Herbert E. Dawson.)

Right—First Methodist, Buffalo, Johnson County. Constructed in 1899, the First Methodist Church is an excellent example of manufactured architecture with its machine-made ornamental detail.

Saint Anthony's, Casper, Natrona County.
Saint Anthony's Church, a Garbutt and Weidner design, has a very distinctive appearance with the tall bell tower, tile roof and decorative brickwork.

also used to house local schools or libraries.

A community's size and monetary means, as well as religious needs, determined the type of church that was erected. Often the parishioners' wealth was expressed in the type of church that was constructed. In other instances, churches were simple for doctrinal reasons, not for lack of money. Differences in the ethnic background and the philosophy of denominations were sometimes expressed architecturally and were frequently delineated inside the building.

Foreign immigrants expressed the need for familiar activities in a church setting; their churches were a place where the customs and religious rites that they brought with them could be practiced. In some German-Russian, German, Scandinavian, Hispanic, and Native American churches, religious services were offered in a traditional language until the 1930s. At Saint Paulus Deutsche Evangelische Lutherische Kirche in Laramie, religious services were held in German until 1932. The same was true for the German Lutheran Church in Germania (which was renamed during World War I to become Emblem). Today some services are still offered in the

Saint Joseph's, Rawlins, Carbon County.
The domed tower of Saint Joseph's is easily identified in the Rawlins skyline. The cornerstone was laid in 1915, and the church was occupied in 1916.

original language, especially on the Wind River Reservation. Local services are still held in Spanish and Basque as well. Ethnicity in Wyoming architecture was most apparently expressed in a religious setting. In fact, there is a tendency for ethnic church architecture to survive longer than other types of ethnic architecture.

Architect-designed churches, such as Casper's Saint Anthony's and Rawlins's Saint Joseph's, are architecturally unique. Saint Anthony's square bell tower with a tile roof looks as if it belongs in Italy. Casper architects Garbutt and Weidner assembled a highly distinctive design by integrating the repetitive use of round arches with the square tower.

Saint Joseph's unusual round dome sits atop an octagonal and square tower, and the dome almost resembles an onion dome. Once again the architect chose to use rounded arches over the windows, doors and in the tower as well. Saint Joseph's and Saint Anthony's each have a rose window centered above the entry.

Many of Wyoming's churches, both architect-designed and manufactured, have Gothic Revival origins. The Gothic architecture found in twelfth-century European cathedrals served as an inspiration for many American churches. Some parishioners may have unconsciously chosen the Gothic Revival style of architecture for their church because of its historical associations with European Christianity. Saint Paul's Episcopal Church in Evanston and Buffalo's Methodist Episcopal Church, now the First United Methodist Church, illustrate the nineteenth-century fondness for Gothic Revival architecture in manufactured buildings.

Some religious denominations created architectural guidelines, and even designs, for their practitioners to use when building a church. Some plans or designs were distributed by the church hierarchy and used repeatedly in manufactured church architecture. These guidelines and designs were intended to offer practical and economical ideas on decor as well as interior arrangement.

Constructed in 1899 by local builders, Buffalo's Methodist Episcopal church has numerous machine-made ornamental details, such as the shingles on the tower, the quatrefoil gable ornament and the windows and doors. Saint Paul's

Church in Evanston is a highly decorative example of a frame Gothic Revival church. Builders utilized the pointed arch motif in the lancet windows and barge boards. A quatrefoil window and ornamental details accent this manufactured church.

Some of Wyoming's most picturesque churches are the one-room log churches found in rural areas such as Eden and Esterbrook, near Laramie Peak, that are typical folk churches. Many of Wyoming's first churches were folk one-room buildings; these churches are still common today in rural areas. Saint Hubert the Hunter in Bondurant is a typical folk church constructed by locals. Rounded logs, obtained locally, were connected using saddle notches.

The Auburn Rock Church located in Lincoln County is one of the oldest buildings in the Star Valley. The masonry is rough-cut with irregular coursing and is beautifully executed in this late nineteenth-century church. The building served

as a public meeting place for the community, in addition to its use for religious purposes for the Church of Latter-Day Saints.

The designs painted on Saint Stephen's Church on the Wind River Reservation are symbolic to the Arapaho culture. Although the church itself is most likely architect-designed, the symbols are traditional. The geometric red, black and white designs are typical of the Northern Arapaho; these traditional designs are also found on beaded or painted dance costumes and on traditional artifacts. Ethnicity in this case is not related to the form of the building itself, but instead is conveyed by the decorations.

Included among Wyoming's religious buildings are some of the oldest and most carefully preserved of the state's architecture.

RESIDENTIAL

Wyoming's historic houses are extremely varied. Architect-designed, manufactured and folk houses abound.

Historically, some owners chose to express their wealth and social status by investing in expensive architect-designed buildings with lavish interior appointments. These residences visually communicated the owner's social standing in the community as well as the architectural fashions of the day. The construction materials and designs also represent rather expensive housing stock.

Salt Lake City architect Walter E. Ware designed an elaborate home and carriage house for merchant Edward Ivinson of Laramie. Construction on the Ivinson Mansion began in 1892. The mansion is a wonderful montage of Victorian decorative features. On the facade, a squared tower displays both a bow window on the second floor and paired round-headed windows on the next. The second tower that flanks the front is octagonal and is topped by a conical roof. The building is typical of some late nineteenth-century structures which exhibit a contrast of building materials; the first story is stone while the upper stories are covered with shingles. Manufactured architectural scrollwork decorates the porch. The Ivinsons invested a substantial amount in their distinctive Laramie home.

J. B. Okie of Lost Cabin made his fortune in the sheep industry. Construction on his mansion, known locally as "Big Tipi," began in 1900.

Rock Church, Auburn, Lincoln County.
Constructed during the late nineteenth century in the Star Valley, the beautiful Auburn Rock Church is an important part of Mormon history.

Left—Ivinson Mansion, Laramie, Albany County. Edward Ivinson could afford a well-known architect and the best materials available when he built his substantial home. The Ivinson Mansion, constructed in 1892, is an interesting combination of Victorian architectural elements.

Right —J. B. Okie's Home, Fremont County. Money made in the sheep industry was invested in J.B. Okie's unusual house. The octagonal tower is a dominant feature on the facade.

Historic Governor's Mansion, Cheyenne, Laramie County.
First occupied in 1905 by Governor B.B. Brooks, the
Neoclassical nature of the Historic Governor's Mansion
visually relates the important role of its occupants.

Trail End, Sheridan, Sheridan County.
The Flemish gables in combination with Neoclassical
details give the John B. Kendrick residence, Trail End, a
very distinctive appearance.

Montgomery Ward House, 1916 Montgomery Ward catalog.
The advertisement for this Montgomery Ward house illustrates what type of residential structure was popular in 1916. Manufactured architecture was readily available to people in Wyoming. (Courtesy of the American Heritage Center, University of Wyoming.)

The building represents an interesting mixture of architectural forms and features. The three-story octagonal tower is typical of nineteenth-century architecture, and yet, the rectangular plan and restrained use of ornamental detail is more typical of the twentieth century. Certainly, it resembles no other residence in Wyoming.

Although not as large as the Ivinson or J.B. Okie Mansion, the Historic Governor's Mansion is a substantial architect-designed residence located in Cheyenne. Architect Charles Murdock used Neoclassical details such as the pediment and corinthian columns to help define the important character of the structure. Governor B. B. Brooks first occupied the building in January 1905.

The Kendrick Mansion in Sheridan is also unlike any other Wyoming residence. To many, John B. Kendrick exemplifies the "self-made" man. Kendrick worked first as a cow hand and eventually became Governor and Senator. Kendrick hired Billings, Montana, architect William McAllister to design the exterior of his expensive house in town while D. Everett Waid of New York City designed the interior according to Kendrick's instruction. Construction began in 1908 on the stone mansion known as Trail End. Distinctive Flemish gables flank the Neoclassical entry of Trail End. The architect's combination of Flemish gables and Neoclassical details, topped with a tile roof, make the building unique in Wyoming.

Throughout the nineteenth and twentieth centuries, architects and builders marketed their designs in a variety of publications. The combination of standardized construction materials and commercialized plans produced an endless array of choices in American housing. Historic neighborhoods all over the state illustrate this rich variety of manufactured housing.

Publications advertising house plans were mass produced inexpensively at the end of the nineteenth century. Some of the publications were illustrated with plates showing extensive line drawings of architectural elements such as windows, canopies, porches, towers, molding and interior features. Elevations of the facade and sides of the residences were also shown. Floorplans added another dimension to the pattern book's illustrations.

Crook House, Cheyenne, Laramie County.
Machine-made ornamentation decorates the Crook House built in the late nineteenth century. Attorneys renovated the building during the 1980s, and it is currently used as a law office. *(Drawing by Jamie Wells.)*

Worland House, Worland, Washakie County.
Bungalows were a popular form of housing in Wyoming and throughout the United States. The Worland family chose to construct a bungalow because it was both fashionable and comfortable.

Architects advertised their wares in popular magazines of the period such as the *Ladies' Home Journal*. Buyers could purchase detailed house plans through the mail. Many of the standardized plans featured highly-decorative substantial houses; the Ferris Mansion in Rawlins is a good example of this phenomenon. Other examples exist in the Rainsford and Capitol North neighborhoods in Cheyenne. Property owners continued to use their houses to express their social status.

After the turn of the century, corporations such as Sears and Roebuck, Montgomery Ward, and Aladdin, among others, produced catalogs of pre-cut houses. These mail order catalogs illustrated a front perspective and an interior floorplan; a narrative further described the buildings. Of course, the price of each house was clearly marked. Catalogs of pre-cut houses designed to be assembled on site were exceedingly popular until the depression during the 1930s. Structures such as the Cheyenne foursquare are

Rock Springs House, Sweetwater County. This house, located close to the railroad tracks, is an interesting combination of both folk and manufactured elements. The stonework and the overall plan of the house seem to be folk, but the extensive scroll-sawn ornamentation is manufactured.

representative of the type of houses that were available through the mail.

Lumberyards in Worland advertised in the *Worland Grit*. House plans as well as construction materials could be purchased locally. As a result, Dad Worland had a house built by local contractor H. C. Shirk in 1917. The Worland House is a noteworthy bungalow with typical bungalow features including a gable roof with exposed eaves, a large front porch, and novelty siding punctuated by numerous windows. Aesthetically,

perhaps some of the bungalow's most endearing qualities relate to the interior. Bungalows became such a popular housing type in the twentieth century that a journal titled *The Bungalow Magazine* extolled the virtues of bungalow-living.

Of course, some of Wyoming's houses do not fit neatly into a category of manufactured or folk architecture. A stone house in Rock Springs, located close to the railroad tracks, clearly illustrates the mixture of manufactured materials and folk traditions. Scroll-sawn manufactured details

decorate the porches, bow window and gable while the house's stonework is more typical of a folk house.

Among the first examples of pure folk architecture in Wyoming is the tipi. The tipi is both a historic folk structure and one that is still used today. Historically, tipis were designed as portable buildings. The tipi's conical shape and interior arrangement of poles vary from one tribe to another. Although modern tipis are generally made with manufactured canvas, historically, animal hides covered the exterior. During religious ceremonies as well as social occasions, Native Americans continue to erect tipis and brush arbors for shelter. Unlike most cultures, Native Americans still actively employ traditional designs in their architectural repertoire.

Shotgun houses, which originated in the folk architecture tradition, were some of the first houses built in the state as a result of the construction of the Union Pacific Railroad. Shotguns are characterized by their long narrow shape. Usually they are only one room wide and perhaps two to four rooms deep. A gable roof caps the shotgun, and the facade consists of a door,

Tipis, Portable Dwellings.
Tipis are an example of a continuing folk tradition.
Designed as a portable shelter, tipis are still used today.
(Photo by Fred Chapman.)

window and frequently a simple porch. It is generally believed that the shotgun house has African American origins. Yet corporations soon utilized the form of the shotgun to house their workers because shotguns were inexpensive and simple to construct. Many of Wyoming's shotguns have manufactured details and may have been pre-cut houses that were shipped to the state by rail. So although the shotgun house is folk in origin, some may also fall into the category of manufactured architecture. Neighborhoods in Laramie, Rock Springs and Sheridan all have shotguns which are located close to the railroad tracks.

The log house at the Boswell Ranch in Albany County is a strong example of folk architecture. The hewn logs and carefully crafted full-dovetail notches display a high level of craftsmanship. Constructed during the nineteenth century from materials obtained locally, the Boswell Ranch house illustrates the time-consuming construction of some folk architecture.

When the Bath Family arrived in Laramie, they established a strong tradition of constructing folk buildings of stone. Simple native stone

Far left, upper photograph—
Bath Houses, Laramie, Albany County.
These simple, yet beautiful, stone houses were constructed by the Bath family during the nineteenth century. They are enrolled in the National Register of Historic Places.

Far left, lower photograph—
Bath Ranch, Albany County.
Similar to the houses built in town, the stone buildings at the Bath Ranch exhibit a high level of craftsmanship. Both houses are examples of a folk architecture form known as an I-house.

Left—
Boswell Ranch House, Albany County.
The corner notching on this early two-story log home exhibits a high level of craftsmanship.
(Photo by Mark Junge and Clayton Fraser.)

Sheep Wagons, Rural Wyoming.
Like the tipi, the sheep wagon was a form of portable shelter used in early Wyoming. Some sheep wagons have been replaced by travel trailers, but some continue to serve as convenient, compact housing for sheepherders.

structures including houses and a brewery, as well as a ranch house and barn, all illustrate the technical skill members of the family possessed. Houses in Laramie constructed by members of the Bath family are beautiful one-story residences with minimal decoration constructed with locally quarried stone. Houses at the Bath Ranch outside of Laramie are typical folk houses according to their form and interior plan.

Wyoming communities display historic residences in a range of architectural types and categories from tipis and sheep wagon to mansions, shotguns, and apartment buildings.

TOURISM AND RECREATIONAL Some of
Wyoming's most innovative and interesting historic architecture was generated as a result of the tourist industry. Wyoming's mountains, majestic

The Eaton, Cheyenne, Laramie County.
Not all housing consists of single detached buildings. The Eaton, with its art deco ornamentation, is an attractive apartment building.

Left—Old Faithful Inn, Yellowstone National Park.
Old Faithful Inn is one of Wyoming's most important historic buildings. The design, by noted architect Robert Reamer, the use of native materials, and the setting make Old Faithful a remarkable and immense log building.

Below—Irma Hotel, Cody, Park County.
This native stone building was constructed by Buffalo Bill Cody and named for his daughter Irma. The native stone building was completed in 1902. It is still used as a hotel, and also houses a restaurant and bar.

Howard Hall, Eaton's Dude Ranch, Sheridan County.
The Eaton Brothers are said to have established the first dude ranch in the West. Howard Hall, a recreational center at the ranch, is an unusual log building.
(Drawing by Herbert E. Dawson.)

scenery, cowboy culture and the lifestyle of westerners have always drawn people. Explorers were fascinated by Yellowstone's environment in the early nineteenth century, while later Europeans and Americans came to the territory to hunt buffalo and other game throughout the century. Visitation to the state increased as newspaper accounts, books, and Congressional action in 1872 establishing Yellowstone as a protected area encouraged people to seek the unusual in Wyoming. The reality of living in the West became mixed with the popularization of western life typified by Buffalo Bill's Wild West Show. This mixture of reality and fiction brought tourists to Wyoming in droves.

The tourists needed to be housed, fed and entertained. Entrepreneurs realized that they could capitalize on the growing nineteenth-century tourist industry. Railroad corporations built hotels to accommodate guests on their way to the park as well as accommodations inside the park itself. For example, Northern Pacific Railroad

Johnson House, AMK Ranch, Grand Teton National Park.
Architect-designed, the Johnson house is an elegant
vacation home constructed in 1927. Fine craftsmanship
characterizes the ornamental detailing, such as the
naturally curved log pieces used as porch posts.

Hamilton Store, Old Faithful area, Yellowstone National Park.
Gnarled lodgepole pine logs are skillfully integrated into the unusual porch of the Hamilton store.

hired architect Robert Reamer to construct Old Faithful Inn located close to the geysers in Yellowstone. Buffalo Bill Cody, a businessman as well as a showman, was committed to establishing urban areas in the Big Horn Basin. He constructed the Irma Hotel in Cody in 1902 for tourists on the way to Yellowstone Park as well as for local visitors.

Yellowstone was only one destination for visitors. The image of the cowboy and the West was equally appealing. By the first decade of the twentieth century, the concept of dude ranching began to thrive in the state. The "dude," generally someone from the East who was unfamiliar with western ways, enjoyed western hospitality while helping with chores and exploring Wyoming's impressive landscape. Frequently dude ranches were a mixture of actual working cattle ranches and vacation retreats. The income generated by dudes assisted ranchers during lean times. Of course, the dude was expected to pay for the privilege of staying at the ranch.

The Eaton Brothers along Wolf Creek in northern Wyoming and other early entrepreneurs constructed cabins and recreational buildings

Virginian Hotel, Medicine Bow, Carbon County.
The Virginian, written by Owen Wister and set near Medicine Bow, is one of the landmarks of Wyoming literature. Medicine Bow's largest building is this hotel named for Wister's book. The building, constructed in 1911, is made of ornamental concrete blocks manufactured to resemble stone.

specifically for those dudes who came to vacation in the West. Wealthier dudes actually constructed cabins of their own at Eatons and at other dude ranches so they could return year after year. Howard Hall at Eatons was used as a recreational center for the dude ranch.

By the 1920s, automobiles joined rail lines in providing transportation to tourist sites in Wyoming. Grand Teton National Park, established in 1929 and subsequently enlarged after a great deal of debate, was an additional attraction for visitors. Dude ranches located both inside and outside the current Grand Teton boundaries offered spectacular scenery as well as a Western experience. Surrounding federal forest land also acted as a drawing card for hunters in search of big game.

Architecturally, the buildings designed in response to the tourist industry vary. Wyoming's national parks house some of the largest and most interesting architect-designed structures of the tourist industry, as well as manufactured and folk buildings.

Old Faithful Inn, a National Historic Landmark in Yellowstone National Park, is one of Wyoming's most innovative and spectacular historic buildings. Old Faithful Inn was the first hotel at the park to express a distinctive "Western" character. Architect Robert C. Reamer used native materials such as shingles and logs in a creative manner that is sensitive to the natural surroundings. Constructed in 1903 and 1904, the Northern Pacific Railroad financed the cost. Some look at Old Faithful Inn and see the influence of Swiss chalets because of the prominent gable roof. Others are reminded of the Wyoming mountains by the steeply pitched gable roof, designed to shed snow. The interior of the inn has a majestic rustic lobby that is at least five stories in height. The immense stone fireplace and the gnarled log balconies overlooking the main lobby area gives the interior a very impressive character. Although additions over the years have created more lodging space, generally the Inn's architectural integrity has survived. Fortunately, the National Park Service's dedication during the ravaging fires of 1988 saved the inn and the other historic buildings at Old Faithful.

Commercial enterprises close to the geyser and inn also used native materials. Gnarled

Lake Hotel, Yellowstone National Park.
Recently renovated, Lake Hotel is a substantial frame structure. The Ionic columns and pediment give the building a strong Neoclassical appearance.

lodgepole pine spells out the name of the historic Hamilton Store at the Old Faithful complex.

Other noteworthy architect-designed buildings exist in Yellowstone. Lake Hotel actually predates the construction of Old Faithful Inn. The substantial Neoclassical frame hotel was constructed in 1890 and was also financed by Northern Pacific Railroad. Unlike Old Faithful Inn, Lake Hotel does not reflect its natural majestic setting beside Lake Yellowstone but, instead, expresses a popular architectural style of the time. Recently the hotel, which is one of the largest frame hotels in America, underwent a renovation sensitive to its architecture.

During the early twentieth century, a design ethic existed for the national park system in spite of the fact that not all construction in the national parks was sensitive to the landscape. As the national park system grew, the need for one central agency to administer the parks became apparent. After the creation of the National Park Service as an agency in 1916, a growing influence among architects and government officials articulated the need for the use of native materials. Ultimately a "rustic style," actually based upon log

Museum, Guernsey State Park, Platte County.
The Civilian Conservation Corps utilized native stone in this imaginative building designed by Roland Pray, a National Park Service architect. (Photo by Mark Junge.)

cabin folk architecture, became an important component of NPS architecture. This rustic style was characterized by use of native materials executed in a way that gave the appearance of a hand-crafted structure. The Arts and Crafts Movement, which expressed the need for hand-crafted native construction materials, influenced the design process as did other factors.

During the Depression, when a great deal of new construction was started due to federally sponsored programs, the need to standardize what had already been occurring in the parks was done with the publication of *Park and Recreation Structures* in 1935. This standardized document explained the necessity of using compatible materials and design within the parks. Subsequent documents highlighted noteworthy Wyoming buildings such as the Museum at Guernsey State Park designed by Park Service architect Roland Pray. This masonry museum, completed in 1939, illustrates an emphasis on small-scaled low structures and hand-crafted stone.

Yet architect-designed buildings were not the only type of tourism-related buildings. Sears and Roebuck marketed a variety of vacation cottages typical of manufactured architecture. Generally the vacation cottages were simple one-story buildings with minimal ornamentation. Vacation cottages around Old Faithful Inn, although not designed by Sears and Roebuck, still illustrate that straightforward or utilitarian appearance. Architects working in both the residential as well as commercial realm began designing standardized gasoline service stations also.

Tourism continued to grow in economic importance to Wyoming as Americans purchased automobiles. The automobile gave tourists freedom to explore new areas; businesses responded to tourists' needs by offering necessary services. A specific type of architecture, generally referred to as roadside architecture, developed in response to auto travel to entice travelers off the highway. Large signs advertised various commercial enterprises such as restaurants, filling stations and motor courts. The abandoned gas station in Douglas is a good example of roadside architecture, as is the Log Cabin Motel in Pinedale.

Folk architecture also plays a role in recreational architecture. The use of readily available

Left—Antelope Station, Douglas, Converse County.
During the teens and twenties service stations became
necessary as automobile traffic became common. The
Antelope Station is long abandoned.

Above—Log Cabin Motel, Pinedale, Sublette County.
The Log Cabin Motel is another example of the roadside
architecture which grew up because of automobile travel.

Grandstands, Buffalo Rodeo Grounds, Johnson County.
Rodeos are important to both tourism and agriculture. Several rodeo structures are now old enough to be considered historic architecture.

materials such as logs was a key component to folk architecture. One of Wyoming's most fanciful examples of folk architecture is found at the HF Bar Dude Ranch in Johnson County. The HF Bar is listed on the National Register of Historic Places because of the variety of historic structures associated with the dude ranch industry. The House that Jack Built is a tourist cabin that grew along with the number of family members.

Reputedly a Mormon family spent summers at the HF Bar each year, and they expanded the cabin's space to fit the family's increasing size.

Wyoming's recreation and tourist industry, which does not seem to follow the boom and bust cycles of some of Wyoming's other industries, has produced some of the most unique structures in the state. Interesting recreational buildings continue to be constructed.

HF Bar Dude Ranch, Johnson County.
This historic dude ranch gave guests the opportunity to construct their own cabins. Wyoming's scenery attracts multitudes of tourists.

CHAPTER SIX

Preserving Wyoming's Buildings

Historic preservation in a state as young as Wyoming is a challenge. Certainly the task of preserving buildings is difficult nearly anywhere in the United States. Yet from a preservationist's perspective, Wyoming is a rich state where some of the oldest buildings, such as the structures at Fort Laramie or the Sun Ranch in Natrona County, continue to stand.

Unlike more populous areas, Wyoming still retains elements of its original pre-development landscape. Although changes in vegetation and wildlife have occurred, as well as small-scale urbanization, a great deal of the landscape remains unaltered in this primarily rural state. In essence, part of the settlement landscape still remains. Wyoming is fortunate because in many areas, especially along the American east and west coasts,

Left—
Ranch near Chugwater,
Platte County.
Many parts of Wyoming retain elements of the settlement era. This stone ranch house is dwarfed by the massive bluffs found in the Chugwater area.

the original look and feel of the area is long gone.

Some of Wyoming's most impressive sites are a combination of natural and historic environments. Places such as the LX Bar Ranch in Campbell County and the HF Bar Dude Ranch in Johnson County are aesthetically pleasing as well as historically important. Picturesque small towns, such as Jay Em in Niobrara County or Lost Cabin in Fremont County, offer a sense of a less complicated time. Bear Creek Valley in Goshen County and the rural area around the town of Chugwater are more than pretty places; residents of both areas still have a strong sense of community. Aesthetics, history, and a sense of community are all important elements of historic preservation.

Historic preservation enhances our quality of life. Neighborhoods such as the South Wolcott Historic District in Casper or the Rainsford Historic District in Cheyenne immediately relay information on the social and cultural history of the cities. Historic commercial districts in Sheridan and Evanston are tangible connections to those cities' prosperous pasts. Additionally, historic storefronts provide pleasant streetscapes with attractive amenities. Some cities visually describe the boom and bust cycle that plagues Wyoming's economy. Historic buildings are among the most visible clues to the state's past.

Frequently a town's identity involves its historic core of buildings. Some American cities and towns look virtually the same because of the standardization of construction plans. A McDonald's or Wal-Mart in Cheyenne may be identical to commercial outlets in New Jersey. Alternatively, preserved historic buildings and locales, such as the Sheridan Inn and the Evanston Depot Square project, provide a community with an easily recognizable, distinctive identity.

The process of preserving historic buildings helps to mitigate change, especially during Wyoming's "boom" periods. By preserving our ties to the past, change becomes more bearable; in essence, the change or modernization need not overwhelm residents. It becomes more difficult to discuss historic preservation when a municipality is in the midst of an economic boom because existing facilities are taxed to the limit to provide necessary services. Perhaps one of the advantages of a slower period of growth is that citizens

Boucvalt-Gras House, Rock Springs, Sweetwater County.
Purchased by Roy Boucvalt, this bungalow is one of the few
older homes in Rock Springs that has escaped the ravages
of boom and bust changes. The unusual porch and the
building's unchanged condition enabled the structure to be
enrolled in the National Register of Historic Places.

have the time and energy to identify a community's historic resources and develop a plan for their protection.

As the world's natural resources become depleted, conservation of existing facilities will become increasingly important for economic reasons. Some construction materials are no longer manufactured or quarried and alternative materials may be exorbitantly expensive. Historic log buildings constructed from substantial virgin timber are now irreplaceable. The tie hacks who carefully notched intricate log corners are too old to continue their craft. Some of the craftsmanship that is an integral part of many historic buildings is also irreplaceable.

The economics of preservation goes beyond the cost of replacement. Historic sites have economic potential since tourism is a very significant part of the Wyoming's economy. For example, the Historic State Penitentiary in Rawlins offers an incomparable experience; the look, feel, and even smell of prison life still remain! Wyoming's forts offer a glimpse into the conflicts of the past. Marketing studies indicate that authentic, well-interpreted, historic sites draw visitors.

Left—
Whipple House pre-restoration, Cheyenne, Laramie County.
Before restoration, the Whipple house had lost its porch and some of its stained glass windows and was in desperate need of tender loving care. The property was endangered until the Beierles purchased the building in the early 1980s.

Right—
Whipple House after restoration.
After restoration, the house is transformed into a nineteenth-century beauty. The porch was carefully reconstructed using historic photographs and clues from the building.

Projects like the Whipple House in Cheyenne, where the building was accurately and lovingly restored by Betty Anne and Leonard Beierle, visually illustrate the past and provide a ambience often lacking in newly-constructed buildings. Although the restaurant housed in the building after renovation has closed, the restoration enhanced the building's value as either a business place or a residence.

Other economic development projects include the conversion of historic residential and commercial buildings into office space. Throughout the 1980s, federal historic preservation tax credits motivated Wyoming attorneys to renovate historic buildings in Cheyenne, Sheridan and Thermopolis.

Yet some of the most enthusiastic historic preservationists in Wyoming are home owners and landowners.

Individuals continue to invest time and energy rehabilitating privately-owned historic homes. For example in the early 1980s, it was unusual to see houses with elaborately painted ornamental details; however, now it is common to see lively colors highlighting historic neighborhoods.

Some landowners, as well, take pride in preserving historic structures. Many ranchers conserve natural sites and protect historic structures long after their practical uses no longer exist.

Today, historic preservation is a combination of governmental, private and non-profit efforts. For information about Wyoming's historic preservation activities, contact the State Historic Preservation Office (SHPO) in Cheyenne [*see* "Suggested Readings"] or your local historic preservation commission. Historic preservation commissions are active in several cities, towns and counties throughout Wyoming. These organizations are active participants in historic preservation at the local level.

For more detailed information about governmental preservation efforts contact the SHPO and ask for a copy of the "Wyoming's Historic Preservation Comprehensive Plan" by Rheba Massey. Threats to Wyoming's historical, architectural, and archaeological resources are identified in the plan with suggestions for preserving sites in the state.

Free brochures and technical architectural information are available from the SHPO and the

Tax Act Project, Sheridan, Sheridan County.
Attorneys renovated the commercial building on the left of the photograph with the ornate keystone and decorative brick window surrounds. A modern storefront was removed and the building changed from a bakery into an office building. Millions of dollars have been invested in private preservation projects, like this one, during the 1980s.

National Park Service. Information about the National Register of Historic Places is also available from the SHPO.

The National Trust for Historic Preservation offers a wide variety of services including publications, newsletters and grant funds.

The section "Suggested Readings" at the end of this book lists addresses for these agencies.

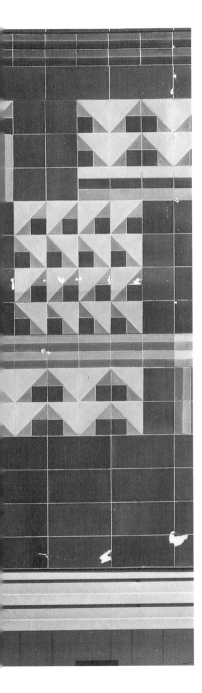

Left—
Commercial Building,
Rawlins, Carbon County.
This building illustrates an example of decorative ceramic tile. Once covered by a metallic front, the continuous Wyoming wind removed the covering and revealed this elaborate tile advertisement.

CHAPTER SEVEN

Describing Wyoming's Historic Buildings

Sometimes it is important to record detailed architectural information about a building. For example, if a structure is to be nominated to the National Register of Historic Places, the building must be described architecturally so that the written communication accurately depicts the structure. In other instances, writing architectural descriptions helps to determine the important components of a building's design. When a building is closely observed sometimes interesting, previously unnoticed architectural features suddenly reveal themselves. Carefully recorded observations can clarify construction techniques of the period, the types of building materials available, and how the building evolved or changed over the years.

The following will offer a systematic approach to describing Wyoming's historic buildings.

INSTRUCTIONS   It is important to obtain the property owner's permission before walking around the building. Property owners rightfully expect to know when someone enters their property and for what purpose. Sometimes property owners are rather suspicious and tend to think that close observation of a structure is directly linked to the building's monetary appraisal. Owners may ask if you represent the local tax assessor. Usually property owners react positively to architectural inquiries once they realize their taxes will not increase.

It is important to walk completely around the structure to determine the original appearance of structure, the size and the plan. Additions may have changed the appearance of the building, and these need to be noted.

Consider the setting when you observe the structure. The following questions are pertinent to describing the character of the building and the area:

• Is the building in an urban or rural location?

• Is the area primarily residential, commercial, industrial, agricultural, or institutional?

• Is the building under study surrounded by other structures which are similar or related?

• Is it located in a complex of related buildings? If so, how are the buildings arranged?

• Was the building intentionally placed by the builder to shelter it from the weather?

• Are there other noteworthy man-made or natural features in the area?

• What type of vegetation surrounds the building?

Each side of a building must be analyzed and described in a systematic manner. Start with the front, called the facade. After describing the entire facade, proceed to each side of the structure. Describe the foundation first and then describe the first story, next the second, moving upward. Follow the same pattern for each side of the building as you record the details.

Access to the interior, always a plus, allows the surveyor to record the floor plan and determine how the building was actually used. If possible, it is important to record the interior as well as the exterior

The Wyoming State Historic Preservation Office (SHPO) has developed a form to assist people in describing a structure. The form offers a

Arcade, Rock Springs, Sweetwater County. Describing architecture is made easier by studying buildings which illustrate certain architectural elements. This Rock Springs house shows a good example of an arcade, a series of round arches supported by columns.

step-by-step approach to writing architectural descriptions. To obtain a free copy of that form, please contact the SHPO [address listed in appendix]. For additional information refer to the glossary and the section of illustrated architectural elements. The terminology and illustrations will help identify individual building components. As with many professions, architecture has a language of its own. Sometimes the words used to describe a building may seem awkward or cumbersome at first, but don't be intimidated.

Three examples will guide the reader through an architectural description: a description of a residence, a description of a public building, and a description of a log barn.

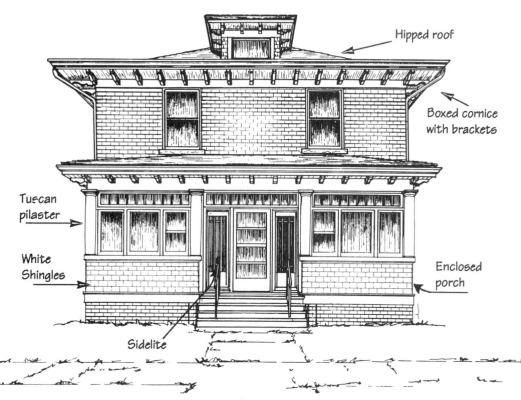

Hipped roof

Boxed cornice with brackets

Tuscan pilaster

White Shingles

Enclosed porch

Sidelite

Architectural Description of a Foursquare

The two-story red brick house located in an older residential neighborhood in Cheyenne is a substantial middle-class residence built in the early part of the twentieth century. It is typical of a type of residence that is sometimes referred to as a foursquare or Prairie Cube.

The structure has a rectangular plan with a brick one-story, rectangular appendage on the rear of the building.

North side: The facade, which faces north, is symmetrical. A brick foundation laid in stretcher bond supports the porch. Steps centered in the middle of the facade lead to an enclosed porch, painted white. A metal storm door with four lites, probably of recent manufacture, is the entry into the enclosed porch. Two sidelights flank the storm door. The bottom third of the porch is covered with white shingles while the upper two thirds consists of windows and tuscan pilasters.

Windows on either side of the entry are grouped in threes. On each side, one of the windows is double hung while the remaining two are stationary and are divided by mullions. The tuscan pilasters flank either side of the window grouping. A string of multi-lite stationary windows surmounts the windows and doors. A boxed cornice with brackets provides ornamentation above the porch. The porch roof is hipped and is covered with asphalt shingles.

The second story displays the red brick laid in stretcher bond. Two identical double hung windows, one lite over one lite, with roughcut sandstone lug sills are symmetrically placed on the facade. The boxed cornice with brackets appears to flair when viewed from the street. A hipped dormer covered with white shingles with one stationary sash is centered on the hipped roof. The dormer also has enclosed eaves and brackets. The roof is covered with asphalt shingles, and the roof is medium pitched.

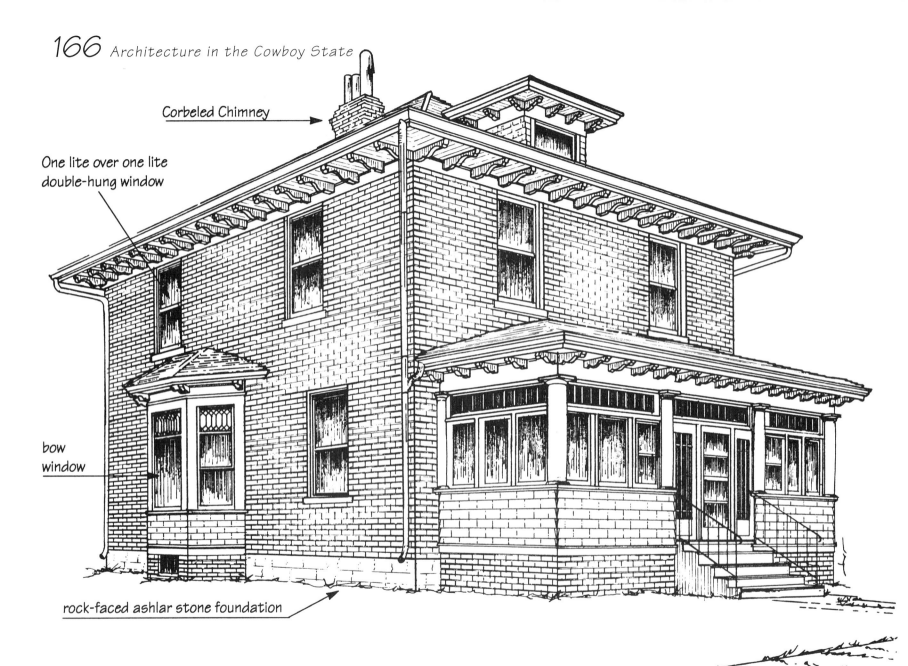

Corbeled Chimney

One lite over one lite
double-hung window

bow
window

rock-faced ashlar stone foundation

East Side: The east side of the residence is not symmetrical. The foundation consists of coursed rock-faced ashlar stone. A bow window with three double hung windows is the prominent feature on the east wall. The windows in the bow window are divided into three parts, the lower two parts are movable while the upper leaded glass is stationary. Horizontal wood siding is part of the lower part of the bow window. A pyramidal roof tops the bow window structure. An additional double hung window with a stone lug sill, one lite over one lite, is located on the first story.

Two identical double hung windows are part of the upper story. The same boxed cornice treatment found on the north side continues to the east elevation.

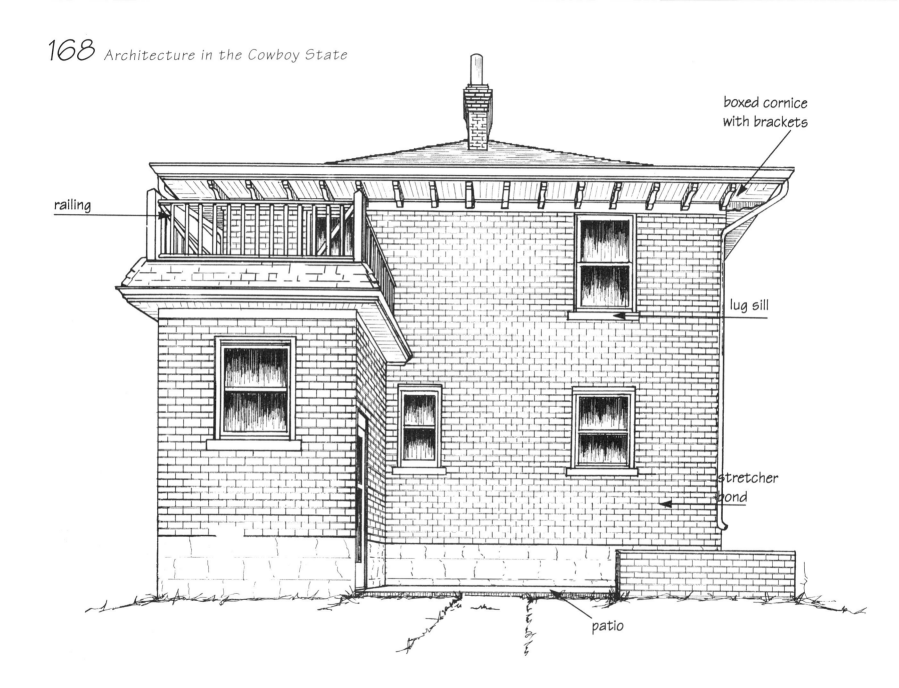

boxed cornice
with brackets

railing

lug sill

stretcher
bond

patio

South Side: The coursed rock-faced stone foundation is evident on the south facade. A one-story projection is found on the southwest part of the structure, and it covers approximately one third of the rear elevation. This projection appears to be original. The projection has a one lite over one lite double hung window with the same type of lug sill as the rest of the house. A metal storm door is located on the east side of the projection which provides access to the back of the house. The projection is topped by a railing and the structure is used as a deck.

A poured concrete patio is located beside the rear of the structure. The main building has two different size double hung windows on the first story with the identical type of lug sill as previously described. The same type of double hung window is also found on the second story. A second-story door provides access to the deck.

The same boxed cornice with brackets continues on the rear. A corbeled brick chimney with three metal stacks sits on the rear hip of the roof.

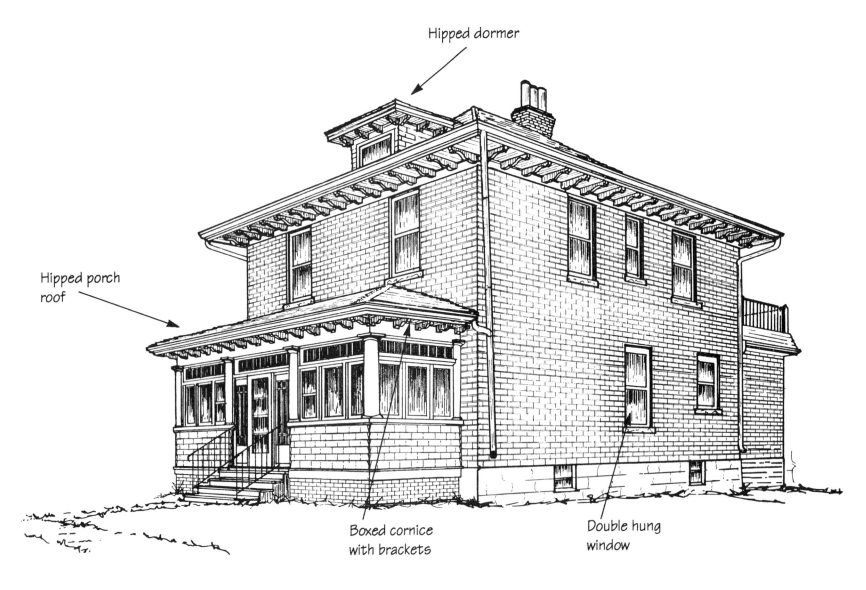

Hipped dormer

Hipped porch roof

Boxed cornice with brackets

Double hung window

West Side: The west side of the building is not symmetrical. The coursed rock-faced stone foundation is the same as previously mentioned. Two different size double hung windows, one lite over one lite, also have sandstone lug sills. The second story has two larger double hung windows flanking a smaller double hung fixture. All the sash are one lite over one lite. The cornice treatment is the same as the other sides.

Conclusion: This residential structure remains unchanged from its original construction with the exception of the addition of metal storm doors. The building has been carefully maintained by its owners and is a strong contributor to the Rainsford Historic district.

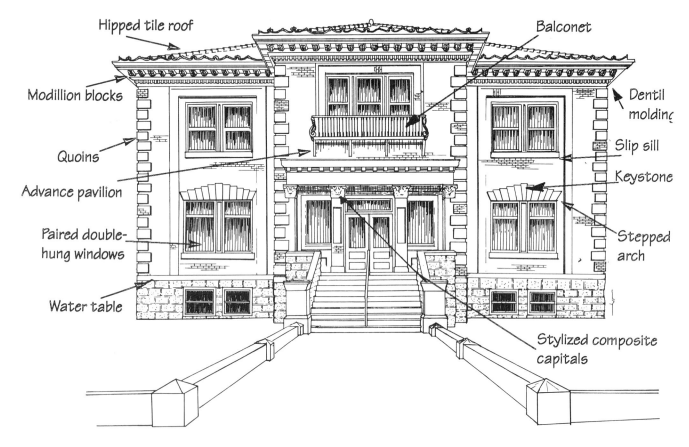

Hipped tile roof

Modillion blocks

Quoins

Advance pavilion

Paired double-hung windows

Water table

Balconet

Dentil molding

Slip sill

Keystone

Stepped arch

Stylized composite capitals

Albany County Public Library

This second example, an architectural description of the historic Albany County Public Library, is shorter, but describes only the front elevation or facade.

The Carnegie Library, constructed in 1905, is a domineering two-story red brick building. Located along Grand Avenue in Laramie, the former library's ornate Neoclassical details and impressive stature give the building a distinctive architectural character among the city's public buildings.

Constructed with a rectangular plan, a two-story central advance pavilion centered on the facade focuses attention on the building's entry. The foundation consists of rusticated stone laid in regular courses. Four double-hung windows furnish light to the basement. A stone water table delineates the separation between the foundation and the first story.

As part of the central entry, a poured concrete straight staircase with large concrete piers provides access to the building's main entry on the first story. The recessed entry as part of a portico is located behind four square brick columns with stylized composite capitols. The library's double doors are wood paneled with one stationary sash in each door. A transom and a large stationary window on either side of the doors are important elements in the entry. A painted metal entablature with dentil molding is placed directly above the composite capitols. One set of paired double-hung windows, one lite over one lite, with a concrete stepped arch and a keystone is located on either side of the advance pavilion. Slip sills are found at the bottom of the windows. Molded brick surrounds frame the first and second story windows on the facade. The brick is laid in a stretcher bond.

The windows on the second story are also paired, and double hung; each set has a slip sill similar to those on the first story. The fixture above the brick columns in the central block is grouped as a triple window and has an iron balconet. Molded brick surrounds group the three double hung sash. Brick quoins at each corner of the library provide further ornamental relief to the building.

Dentil molding, egg and dart molding and modillion blocks add a classical flair to the building's boxed cornice. A decorative metal roofscreen accents the medium pitched red tile hipped roof.

A short concrete wall surrounds the lot where the building sits. Through the years few changes were made to the library, so the building retains its original appearance.

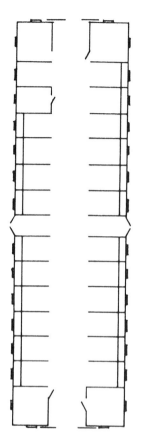

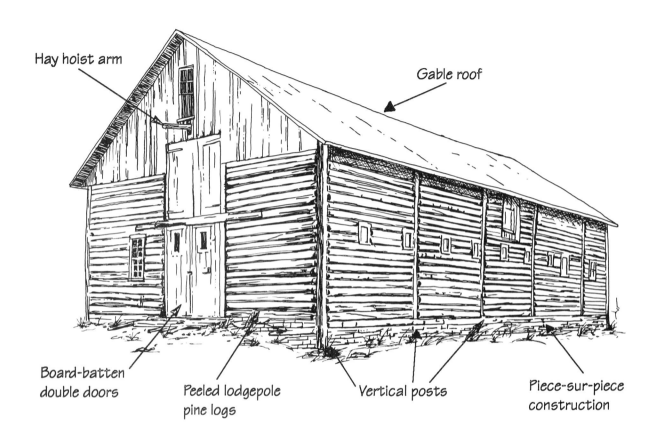

Hay hoist arm

Gable roof

Board-batten double doors

Peeled lodgepole pine logs

Vertical posts

Piece-sur-piece construction

Floor plan, Rock Dale Barn.

This typical piece-sur-piece barn floor plan illustrates how the stalls divide the barn's interior. When recording buildings, it is important to measure and document the interior of the structure. *(All illustrations in Chapter Seven are by Jamie Wells.)*

Rock Dale Barn

The historic barn found at the old Rock Dale Stage Station located along the Overland Trail is an unusual type of log structure. This description details what is shown in the photograph and line drawing, but does not deal with the entire building.

Several immense log barns dot the landscape on the Laramie Plains. The barn found at Rock Dale is one of the oldest and most distinctive piece-sur-piece buildings in Wyoming. The builder was highly skilled, and the barn exhibits a high level of craftsmanship. The barn was originally constructed primarily as a horse barn. Log corrals surround the barn.

Constructed during the late nineteenth century, the log barn at Rock Dale consists of peeled lodgepole pine logs probably harvested in the surrounding mountains. The building's plan is rectangular, and the barn is approximately two tall stories in height. It measures 35 feet by 80 feet.

The foundation consists of roughcut sandstone laid in courses. A sill log sit on top of the sandstone.

The primary entry is centered on the east side, a gable end, through double board and batten doors. These doors slide horizontally. A single stationary sash in each door provides some illumination for the barn's interior. Flanking the double doors on one side is a six multi-lite over six multi-lite double-hung window with frame surrounds.

Above the double board and batten doors are frame double doors with metal strap hinges that provides entry into the hay loft. Above the hay loft doors is a hay hoist arm used to assist in lifting hay into the loft. At the top of the facade is a double hung window with only the top sash, consisting of four lites, remaining. Board and batten material was used above the logs in the gable end.

Vertical log posts are located at the corners and are spaced every twelve to nineteen feet along the side. These vertical logs are grooved, and the horizontal logs fit into the grooves. This log construction technique is known as piece-sur-piece. Chinking is used to fill in the spaces between the logs.

The north side of the barn is divided into five sections and each section, except the last one, has

two small stationary windows that provide light for the stalls inside. The last section only has one window. Another hay loft door, placed in the center of the north side's second story, provides an additional exterior entry for the loft.

The large gable roof, now covered with corrugated metal roofing, provides shelter for the barn. With the exception of the roofing material, the Rock Dale barn remains unaltered.

Glossary

Arcade—A series of rounded arches supported by columns. *See* photograph, p. 163.

Ashlar—Squared building stone. *See* stone finishes and courses, Architectural Elements, Appendix B.

Balconet—A false balcony constructed with a low railing outside a window.

Balcony—A projection from an upper story window or door surrounded by railing.

Bay window—A window that projects from the building with at least three sections. *See* windows, Architectural Elements, Appendix B.

Board and Batten—An exterior frame cladding material used on the sides and roofs of buildings consisting of vertical boards covered at the seams with smaller boards referred to as battens. *See* exterior finishes, Architectural Elements, Appendix B.

Ceramic Tile—Fired clay tile used as decoration on building exteriors. *See* photograph, p. 160.

Chinking—Material, sometimes mud or concrete, used to fill holes between logs or other exterior finishes.

Composite capital—The top part of a column with a mixture of elements from an Ionic capital and a Corinthian capital. *See* columns, Architectural Elements, Appendix B.

Conical roof—A roof shaped as a cone. Conical roofs are frequently found on towers. *See* roofs, Architectural Elements, Appendix B.

Corinthian capital—The top part of a column characterized by large acanthus leaves. *See* columns, Architectural Elements, Appendix B.

Corner notching—The manner in which logs are joined or notched at the corner of a log building. *See* log notches, Architectural Elements, Appendix B.

Cornice—The top molding or projection in a wall that caps or crowns the wall. *See* ornamentation, Architectural Elements, Appendix B.

Cruciform—Shaped like a cross.

Dentil—Molding characterized by small square blocks, like teeth. *See* ornamentation, Architectural Elements, Appendix B.

Dormer—A window that projects from the roof. *See* dormers, Architectural Elements, Appendix B.

Dovetail notching—Corner notching or joining, can be full or half-dovetail. Dovetail notching takes a substantial amount of skill to execute. *See* log notches, Architectural Elements, Appendix B.

Dugout—A shelter, sometimes rather crude, where the earth has literally been dug out or removed from the hillside. Sometimes dugouts were the first shelter constructed before more permanent, above ground, lodging could be constructed. *See* photograph, p. 25.

Eaves—The lowest, projecting, part of a sloped roof.

Egg and dart molding—A type of molding in which an egg shape alternates with a dart shape. *See* ornamentation, Architectural Elements, Appendix B.

Facade—Primary or front elevation of a building.

False front—Building constructed with a tall parapet wall on the front that extends beyond the peak of the roof. *See* photographs.

Flemish gables—Curvilinear gables reminiscent of Flemish construction. *See* photograph of Trail End, p. 127.

Flying buttress—Found in Gothic and less frequently in Gothic Revival architecture. Manner in which the load of a roof or vault is transferred from the upper wall to an exterior arch or buttress.

Foursquare—Common twentieth-century house type characterized by its square or nearly square shape. *See* manufactured architecture, Chapter Three.

Frieze—A band, can be decorative or plain, found below the cornice.

Gable roof—A roof shaped like an upside-down V. *See* roofs, Architectural Elements, Appendix B.

Garland—An ornamental detail in the shape of a band of flowers.

Guilloche molding—Molding resembling twisted rope. *See* ornamentation, Architectural Elements, Appendix B.

Hewn—Cut or shaped log with an ax.

Hipped roof—A roof with four pitches. *See* roofs, Architectural Elements, Appendix B.

Ionic column—A column with a capital having spiral shaped designs. *See* columns, Architectural Elements, Appendix B.

Iron front—Also called a sheet metal front. Popular metallic storefront pieces ordered from a catalog for decorative and structural purposes. *See* photograph, Ramrod Gun Shop, p. 46.

Keystone—A wedge shaped stone found in the center of some arches.

Lancet window—A window with a pointed arch typically found in Gothic architecture. *See* windows, Architectural Elements, Appendix B.

Lintel—A structural member, horizontal, that spans openings.

Lites—An individual pane of glass. Also spelled lights.

Lug sill—A sill that extends beyond the bottom of the window. *See* sills, Architectural Elements, Appendix B.

Modillion blocks—Ornamental blocks or brackets found under the cornice. *See* ornamentation, Architectural Elements, Appendix B.

Mullion—A vertical piece or member separating two or multiple windows. *See* windows, Architectural Elements, Appendix B.

Neoclassical—New or reuse of classical orders and details.

Notched corners—Manner in which horizontal logs are joined at the corner. *See* log notches, Architectural Elements, Appendix B.

Novelty siding—A type of horizontal frame siding. *See* exterior finishes, Architectural Elements, Appendix B.

Parapet Wall—Part of a wall that extends beyond the roof. Term used to describe false fronts.

Pavilion—A projection on an exterior wall usually in the center or end of a building.

Pediment—A triangular gable end of the roof above the cornice. *See* photograph, Laramie Masonic Temple, p. 36.

Piece-sur-piece construction—Log construction technique found in military and agricultural architecture. Characterized by horizontal log members fitting into vertical posts. *See* folk architecture, Chapter Three.

Pier—Square pillar or post support. *See* porches, Architectural Elements, Appendix B.

Pilaster—A half column or pier attached to a wall frequently with a capital and base.

Pointed arch—An arch with a point at the apex.

See window and door surrounds, Architectural Elements, Appendix B.

Portico—A porch supported by columns. *See* porches, Architectural Elements, Appendix B.

Pyramidal roof—A hipped roof, resembling an Egyptian pyramid. *See* roofs, Architectural Elements, Appendix B.

Quatrefoil—Ornamental detail consisting of a pattern of four rounded elements.

Quoins—Blocks used in brick or stone buildings at the corner. A quoin can be used for both structural and decorative purposes. *See* photograph, Albany County Library, p. 173

Saddle Notch—Log notching technique less difficult to execute than a dovetail notch. *See* log notches, Architectural Elements, Appendix B.

Sill—The bottom member of a window or door. Also the log that sits on the foundation known as the sill log.

Slip sill—Type of window sill that "slips" into place. *See* sills, Architectural Elements, Appendix B.

Steeple—A tall tower usually attached to a religious structure.

Stretcher bond—Type of brick bond consisting of only stretcher bricks. *See* brick bonds, Architectural Elements, Appendix B.

Stucco—An exterior finish that may consist of mud, cement, sand and water. *See* photograph, Cooper Mansion, p. 35

Terra Cotta—Fired clay, may be glazed or unglazed, used as an exterior cladding material and highly decorative ornamental details. Comes in a variety of colors. *See* photograph, Casper Women's Club House, p. viii.

V notch—Type of log corner notching characterized by a V. *See* log notches, Architectural Elements, Appendix B.

Water table—A molding or projection on the exterior located at the intersection of the basement and first story. Usually decorative.

Architectural Elements

*All illustrations
in this section are
by Jamie Wells.*

Plans

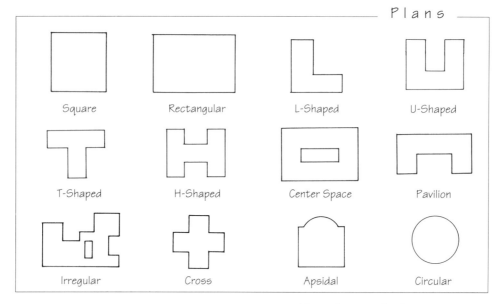

Square   Rectangular   L-Shaped   U-Shaped

T-Shaped   H-Shaped   Center Space   Pavilion

Irregular   Cross   Apsidal   Circular

Number of Stories

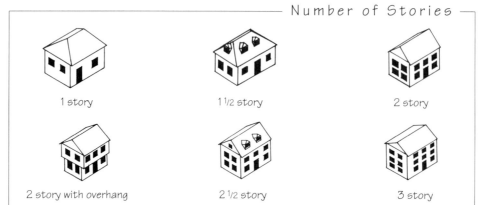

1 story   1 ½ story   2 story

2 story with overhang   2 ½ story   3 story

Basements

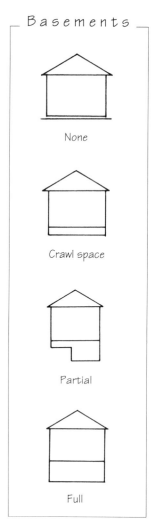

None

Crawl space

Partial

Full

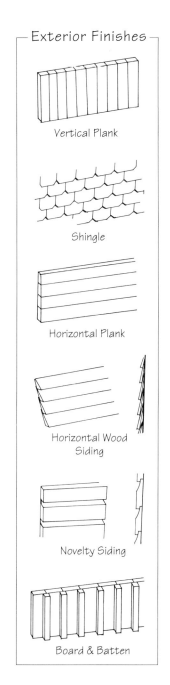

Vertical Plank

Shingle

Horizontal Plank

Horizontal Wood Siding

Novelty Siding

Board & Batten

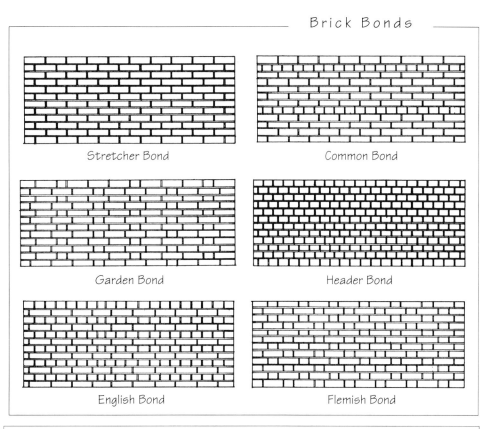

Stretcher Bond

Common Bond

Garden Bond

Header Bond

English Bond

Flemish Bond

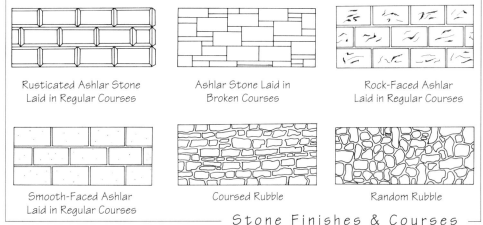

Rusticated Ashlar Stone Laid in Regular Courses

Ashlar Stone Laid in Broken Courses

Rock-Faced Ashlar Laid in Regular Courses

Smooth-Faced Ashlar Laid in Regular Courses

Coursed Rubble

Random Rubble

Stone Finishes & Courses

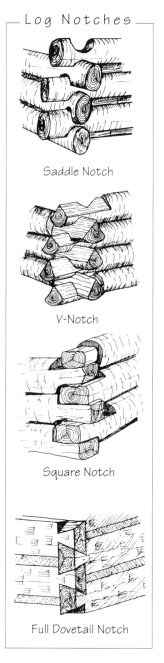

Saddle Notch

V-Notch

Square Notch

Full Dovetail Notch

Shapes of Window & Door Openings

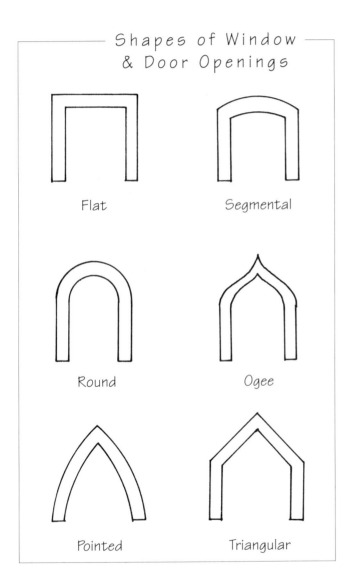

Flat

Segmental

Round

Ogee

Pointed

Triangular

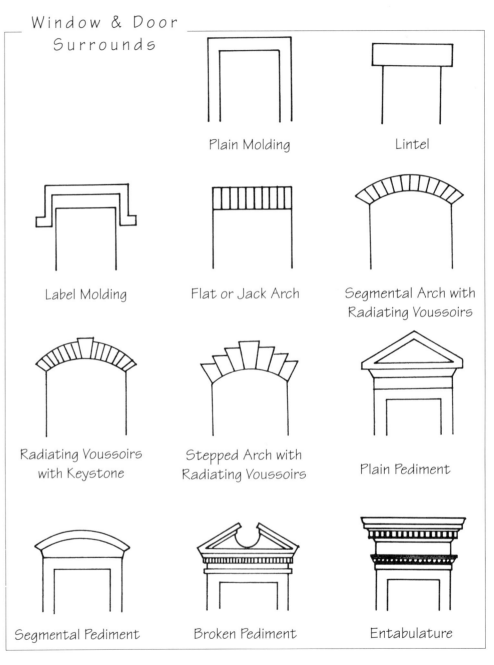

Plain Molding

Lintel

Label Molding

Flat or Jack Arch

Segmental Arch with
Radiating Voussoirs

Radiating Voussoirs
with Keystone

Stepped Arch with
Radiating Voussoirs

Plain Pediment

Segmental Pediment

Broken Pediment

Entabulature

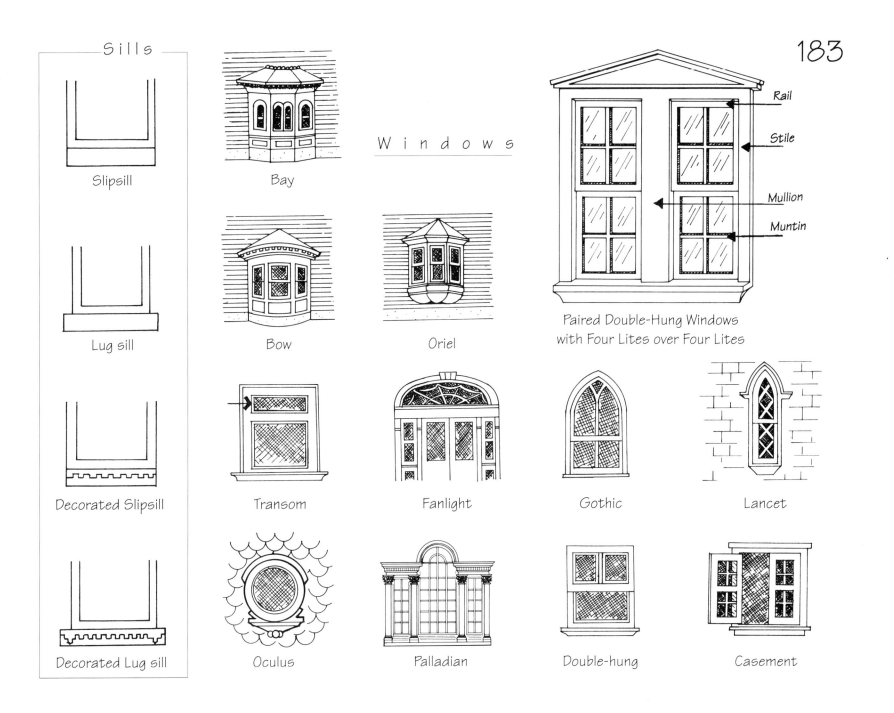

Sills

Slipsill

Lug sill

Decorated Slipsill

Decorated Lug sill

Windows

Bay

Bow

Oriel

Paired Double-Hung Windows
with Four Lites over Four Lites

Rail

Stile

Mullion

Muntin

Transom

Fanlight

Gothic

Lancet

Oculus

Palladian

Double-hung

Casement

R O O F S

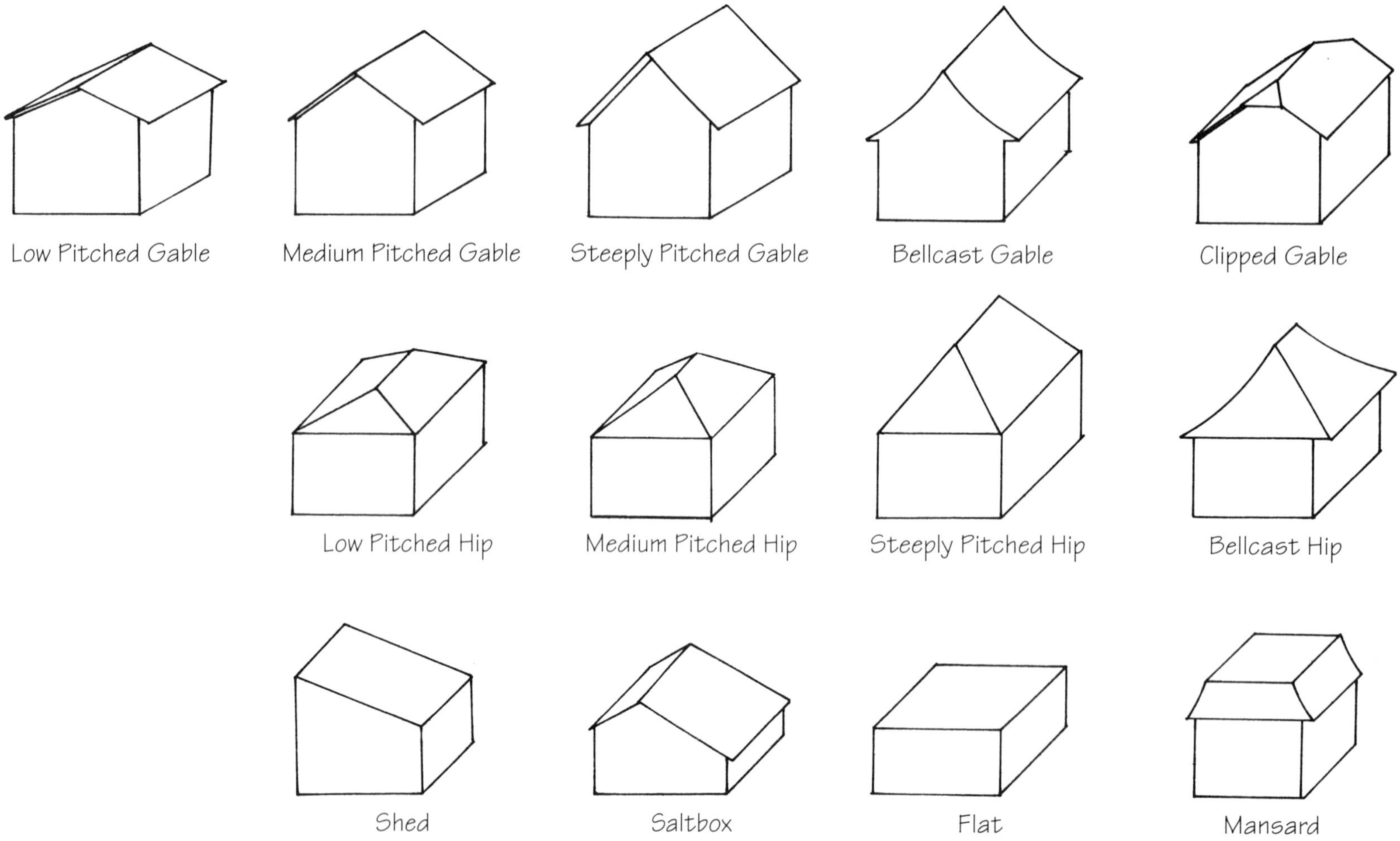

Low Pitched Gable

Medium Pitched Gable

Steeply Pitched Gable

Bellcast Gable

Clipped Gable

Low Pitched Hip

Medium Pitched Hip

Steeply Pitched Hip

Bellcast Hip

Shed

Saltbox

Flat

Mansard

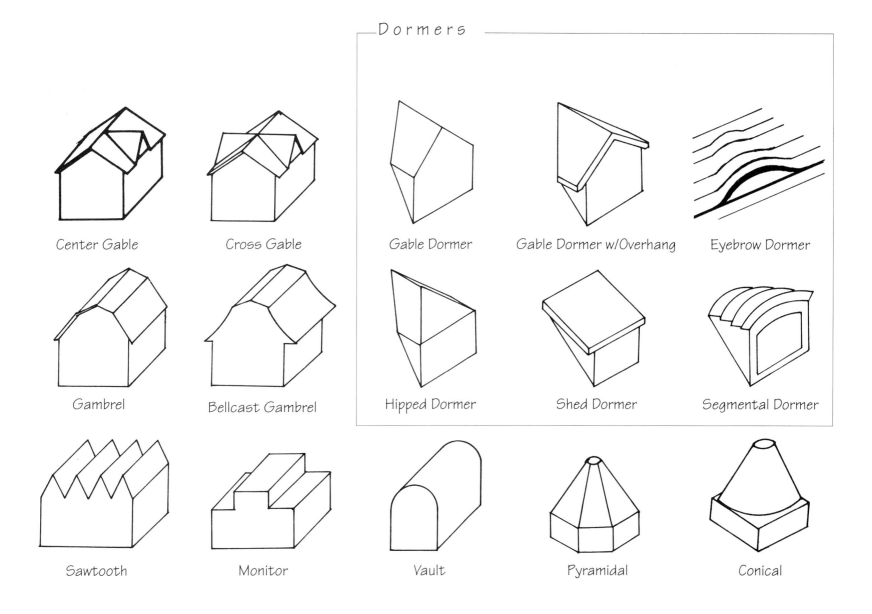

Center Gable

Cross Gable

Dormers

Gable Dormer

Gable Dormer w/Overhang

Eyebrow Dormer

Gambrel

Bellcast Gambrel

Hipped Dormer

Shed Dormer

Segmental Dormer

Sawtooth

Monitor

Vault

Pyramidal

Conical

PORCHES

Stoop

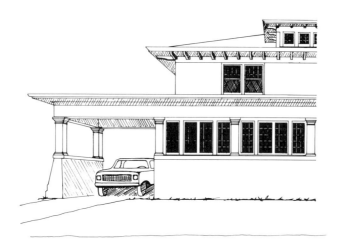

Porte Cochere

Wrap Around Porch

Portico

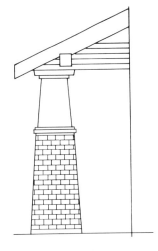

Battered Pier

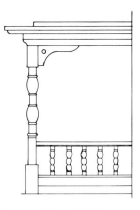

Turned Porch Post

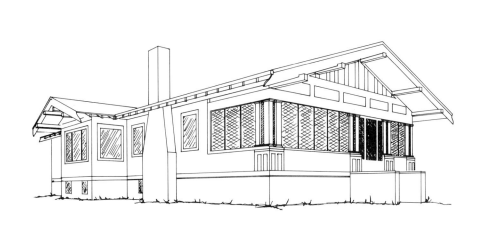

Enclosed Porch

Monumental Portico

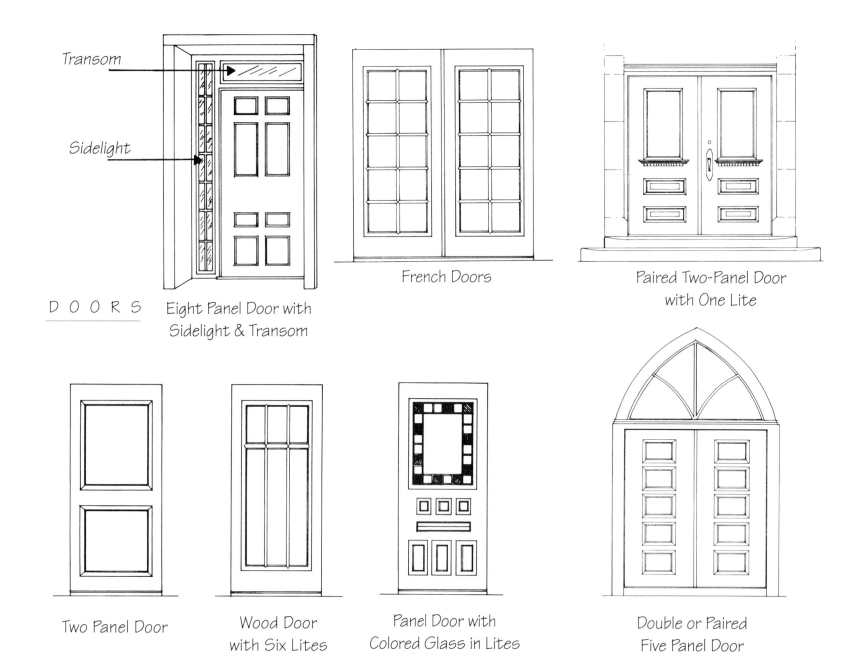

Transom

Sidelight

D O O R S

Eight Panel Door with
Sidelight & Transom

French Doors

Paired Two-Panel Door
with One Lite

Two Panel Door

Wood Door
with Six Lites

Panel Door with
Colored Glass in Lites

Double or Paired
Five Panel Door

Egg and Dart Molding

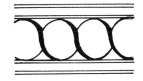

Guilloche Molding

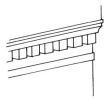

Dentil Molding

Corbel

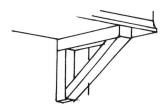

Boxed Cornice
with Brackets

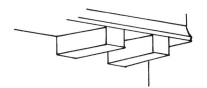

Boxed Cornice
with Dentil Blocks

C o l u m n s

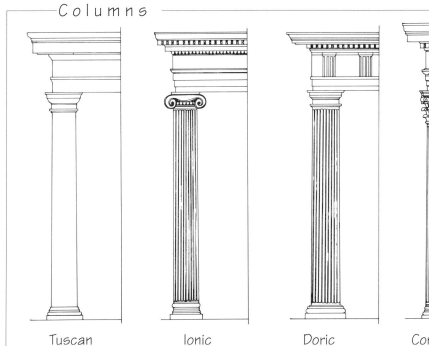

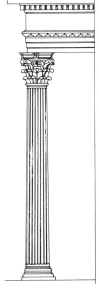

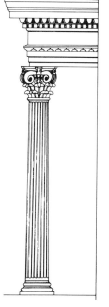

Tuscan   Ionic   Doric   Corinthian   Composite

Console Bracket

Bracket

BIBLIOGRAPHY

Suggested Readings

Foreword

David Kathka refers to Jœl Garreau's book, *The Nine Nations of North America* (Boston: Houghton Mifflin, 1981) in the foreword. Garreau discusses Wyoming in the chapter entitled "The Empty Quarter." Garreau offers a fascinating portrait of Evanston coping with the oil boom of the 1970s.

Ch. 1—The Western Myth and Architecture

Henry Nash Smith's classic study, *Virgin Land: The American West as Symbol and Myth*, (Cambridge, Massachusetts: Harvard University Press, 1950) explores the role myth played in the settlement of the west.

Two articles published in *Annals of Wyoming* discuss the difference between people's perception of Wyoming's heritage and everyday life. Roy A. Jordan and Tim R. Miller wrote "The Politics of a Cowboy Culture" in the Spring 1980 issue (Volume 52, No. 1). Peter Iverson's "Wyoming: Still the Cowboy State?" was published in the Fall 1979 issue (Volume 51, No. 2).

Cowboy Culture: A Saga of Five Centuries (New York: Alfred A. Knopf, 1981) written by David Dary examines the life of the cowboy.

Kingston Wm. Heath analyzes Montana false fronts in his doctoral dissertation, *Striving for Permanence on the Western Frontier: Vernacular Architecture as Cultural Informant in Southwestern Montana* written for Brown University in 1985. (Hopefully this intelligent study will be published as a book.) *Perspectives in Vernacular Architecture, III* edited by Thomas Carter and Bernard L. Herman (Columbia: University of Missouri Press, 1989) contains an article by Heath, "False-Front Architecture on Montana's Urban Frontier."

Certainly Hollywood needs to be acknowledged for its persistent portrayal of the "wild west."

Ch. 2—Architectural Observations

Recently published histories of the American West document the diversity of life and culture during the nineteenth and twentieth centuries. Historians such as Patricia Nelson Limerick in *The Legacy of Conquest: The Unbroken Past of the American West* (New York: W. W. Norton and Company, 1987), Michael P. Malone and Richard W. Etulain in *The American West: A Twentieth Century History* (Lincoln, Nebraska: University of Nebraska Press, 1989) and Robert Athearn in *The Mythic West in Twentieth-Century America* (University Press of Kansas, 1986) all provide foundations for discussing Wyoming's social history and architectural heritage.

The classic study of Wyoming history, *History of Wyoming*, second edition revised (Lincoln: University of Nebraska Press, 1978) written by eminent Wyoming historian, T. A. Larson, is always a useful source of information on Wyoming. *Peopling the High Plains: Wyoming's European Heritage* edited by Gordon Olaf Hendrickson (Cheyenne: Wyoming State Archives and Historical Department, 1977) offers insight into cultural diversity that existed in Wyoming.

National Register files located in the State Historic Preservation Office (SHPO) contain a plethora of information about specific sites. Additionally, information on cultural resource surveys is kept in both the Cheyenne and Laramie offices of the SHPO. *Wyoming: A Guide to Historic Sites* compiled by the Wyoming Recreation Commission (Basin, Wyoming:

Big Horn Publishers, 1976) also contains information about the state's historic sites.

Ch. 3—Interpreting Wyoming's Architecture
Wyoming Architectural Studies

Lack of information about Wyoming's architecture created problems for the Wyoming Historic Preservation Office. To address some of those problems, this book was written. There are only a few sources of information that deal specifically with Wyoming's architecture. As mentioned before, National Register nominations, survey forms and historic contexts frequently contain architectural information.

Judith Hancock Sandoval's *Historic Ranches of Wyoming* (Casper, Wyoming: Nicolaysen Art Museum, 1986) offers insight into Wyoming's agricultural architecture. Robert Rosenberg's historic context "Historic Overview of Ranching to 1890 in Fremont County" written in 1990 explores the architectural differences in ranch architecture. Richard Headlee's unpublished master's thesis, "An Architectural History of Southern Wyoming, 1867-87" written for the University of Wyoming in 1977 discusses some of the state's earliest architecture. Gregory D. Kendrick wrote an article, "Parco, Wyoming: A Model Company Town," for the Spring 1983 edition of the *Annals of Wyoming* (Volume 55, No. 1). Kendrick's article analyzes the history, architecture, and planning that went into the creation of Parco.

Discussion of Wyoming's folk architecture can be found in the *Hoolihan*, a journal published by the Wyoming Folk Arts Program, American Studies Program, University of Wyoming, P.O. Box 4036, Laramie, WY. Folklorist Timothy Evans has written a variety of articles on Wyoming's folk architecture in the *Hoolihan* which was published from 1987 to 1991.

Architectural Walking Tours of Laramie, Wyoming: Tracing the History and Diversity of the Gem City of the Plains written by the Albany County Historic Preservation Board discusses different types of residential buildings found in Laramie. Sheila Bricher-Wade and Betty Anne Beierle wrote a walking tour entitled, *Historic Downtown Cheyenne Walking Tour*. (Other walking tours for cities in the state exist and are equally informative.) *Cheyenne's Historic Architecture*, a booklet prepared by Community Services Collaborative for the Cheyenne-Laramie County Regional Planning Office, explores Cheyenne's architectural history.

The Air Force and its consultant URS Berger produced a multi-volume set entitled *Architectural Survey: F.E. Warren Air Force Base*. The study written in 1984 details the architectural history of the calvary/missile base and is exceedingly informative.

Work's Progress Administration files at the Historical Research Department contain descriptions of Wyoming's architecture and some discussion of Wyoming's architects.

A variety of academic disciplines are involved in the study of historic architecture including history, architectural history, folklore, cultural geography, American studies, and anthropology. Many of the following titles reflect the diversity that exists in the field.

Classic texts discuss American architectural history and architect-designed buildings such as Marcus Whiffen's *American Architecture Since 1780: A Guide to the Styles* (Cambridge, Massachusetts: M.I.T. Press, 1969), Alan Gowans' *Images of American Living: Four Centuries of Architecture and Furniture, A Cultural Expression* (New York: Harper and Row, 1976), Leland Roth's *A Concise History of American Architecture* (New York: Harper and Row Publishers, 1979) and Spiro Kostof's *America by Design* (New York and Oxford:

Oxford University Press, 1987). To find information on the architects who lived and worked in Wyoming, the vertical files at the Historical Research Department, Division of Parks and Cultural Resources, Department of Commerce, must be consulted.

Architecture and Society: Selected Essays of Henry Van Brunt edited by William A. Coles (Cambridge, Massachusetts: Belknap Press of Harvard University Press, 1969) illustrates the creative abilities of architect Henry Van Brunt.

Books written by Jan Jenning and Herbert Gottfried explore the significant role of manufactured architecture (or in their words, industrial vernacular architecture) had in American design. *American Vernacular Interior Architecture: 1870-1940* (New York: Van Nostrand Reinhold Company, 1988) and *American Vernacular Design 1870-1940: An Illustrated Glossary* (New York: Van Nostrand Reinhold Company, 1985) are important works in the field of architectural history. Their pioneering work along with books such as *Houses by Mail: A Guide to Houses from Sears, Roebuck and Company* written by Katherine Cole Stevenson and H. Ward Jandl (Washington, D.C.: Preservation Press, 1986) explore the role of manufactured housing in the twentieth century. *America's Favorite Homes: Mail Order Catalogues as a Guide to Early 20th Century Houses* written by Robert Schweitzer and Michael W.R. Davis (Detroit: Wayne State University Press, 1990) examines the corporations which manufactured pre-built houses. Clay Lancaster's book, *The American Bungalow: 1880-1930* (New York: Abbeville Press, 1985) details the wide variety of houses that were referred to as bungalows.

The American Heritage Center at the University of Wyoming has an interesting collection of Montgomery Ward catalogs for houses as well as a catalog called *The Farm Book*. The catalogs range in date from 1916 to 1925 and illustrate the wide variety of houses that could be purchased from Wards.

Information about the Scandinavian Lutheran Church in Laramie and Wyoming shotguns came from different editions of the *Hoolihan*.

Historian Robert Rosenberg has written a variety of articles, National Register nominations, and books on Wyoming history. Articles such as "Handhewn Ties of the Medicine Bows" published in the *Annals of Wyoming* Spring 1984 (Volume 56, No. 1) explore the role of Scandinavians in the tie industry and the cabins they built for themselves. Rosenberg briefly discusses agricultural and school architecture in *Wyoming's Last Frontier: Sublette County, Wyoming* (Glendo, Wyoming: High Plains Press, 1990).

Author Ted Olson describes the skills of a Swedish log worker in *Ranch on the Laramie* (Boston: Little, Brown and Company, 1973). Little, Brown graciously granted permission to quote from the book. Elinore Pruitt Stewart's *Letters of a Woman Homesteader* reprinted by Houghton Mifflin Company, 1981, describes constructing a homestead cabin in Wyoming.

Regional studies on log architecture include *Log Cabin Studies* by Mary Wilson, published by the United States Forest Service, Department of Agriculture, Ogden, Utah, 1984; Terry Jordan's *Texas Log Buildings: A Folk Architecture* (Austin: University of Texas Press, 1978); and Warren Roberts's *Log Buildings of Southern Indiana* (Bloomington: Trickster Press, 1985).

For more information about folk architecture, books and articles written by Henry Glassie are great sources. *Patterns in the Material Folk Culture of the Eastern United States* (Philadelphia: University of Pennsylvania Press, 1968) and *Folk Housing in Middle Virginia:*

A Structural Analysis of Historic Artifacts (Knoxville: University of Tennessee Press, 1975) are traditional sources of information. Amos Rapoport, in an article in *Buildings and Society: Essays on the Social Development of the Built Environment* (London: Routledge and Kegan Paul, 1980) edited by Anthony D. King, explores the role of cultural baggage in architecture.

Cultural geographer Allen G. Noble's two volume set entitled, *Wood, Brick and Stone: The North American Settlement Landscape* (Amherst: University of Massachusetts Press, 1984) describes the wide variety of folk building forms one finds in the United States. Peter Nabokov and Robert Easton's book, *Native American Architecture* (New York and Oxford: Oxford University Press, 1989) discusses tipis as well as a different types of Native American architecture.

Others sources of information about folk architecture includes the series *Perspectives in Vernacular Architecture*. Camille Wells edited Volumes One (Annapolis: Vernacular Architecture Forum, 1982) and Two (Columbia: University of Missouri Press, 1986) while Thomas Carter and Bernard Herman edited Volume Three (Columbia: University of Missouri, 1989). Additionally *Common Places: Readings in American Vernacular Architecture* edited by Dell Upton and John Michael Vlach (Athens: University of Georgia Press, 1986) contains articles on folk architecture.

Northern Rocky Mountain Architectural Studies

Several books written during the last ten years have expanded our understanding of the historic architecture of the Rocky Mountain West. Thomas Carter and Peter Goss describe house types and architectural styles found in Utah in their book entitled *Utah's Historic Architecture, 1847-1940* (Salt Lake City: University of Utah Press, 1988). *The Grouse Creek Cultural Survey: Integrating Folklife and Historic Preservation Field Research* (Washington, D.C.: American Folklife Center, 1988) written by Thomas Carter and Carl Fleischhauer examines a small Mormon ranching community in Utah from a cultural conservation perspective.

Jennifer Eastman Attebery's *Building Idaho: An Architectural History* (Moscow: University of Idaho Press, 1991) analyzes Idaho's architecture from a historical perspective.

Sarah Jane Pearce describes both types and architectural styles found in Colorado in *A Guide to Colorado Architecture* (Denver: Colorado Historical Society, 1983). *Denver, The City Beautiful and its Architects, 1893-1941* written by Thomas J. Noel and Barbara Norgren in 1987 (Denver: Historic Denver) and *Historic Denver: The Architects and the Architecture* written by Richard Brettell were published by Historic Denver (Denver: Historic Denver, 1973), a non-profit preservation organization. *Bonanza Victorian: Architecture and Society in Colorado Mining Towns* by C. Eric Stoehr (Albuquerque: University of New Mexico Press, 1975) is an interesting examination of nineteenth-century mining towns. *Robert Roeschlaub, Architect of the Emerging West: 1843-1923*, written by Francine Haber, Kenneth R. Fuller and David N. Weitzel, was published by the Colorado Historical Society in 1988.

Although not centered in the Rocky Mountains, *German-Russian Folk Architecture in Southeastern South Dakota* (Vermillion, South Dakota: State Historical Preservation Center, 1984) written by Michael Koop and Stephen Ludwig is a thorough evaluation of German-Russian architecture in South Dakota.

Previously mentioned studies by Mary Wilson and Kingston Heath describe northern Rocky Mountain architecture.

Ch. 4—Wyoming's Architects

Most of the information concerning Wyoming's architects came from the collections of the Historical Research Department and the State Archives located in the Barrett Building in Cheyenne. The U.W. American Heritage Center does have Frederick Hutchinson Porter's collection. A great deal more research remains to be done on the work of Wyoming's architects.

Ch. 5—Historic Themes

National Register nominations and historic survey forms were an integral part of this chapter.

Agriculture

"The Site Arrangement of Rural Farmsteads" by William H. Tishler, *Association for Preservation Technology* (Volume X, Number 1, 1978) compares European farmsteads to American farmsteads.

Two programs supported by the University of Wyoming: the Wyoming Agricultural Experiment Station and the U. W. Extension Office produced informative publications, bulletins, and annual reports for the public that offered information about Wyoming's agricultural architecture.

Community Development

An unpublished article written by Thomas Paul (Baltimore, Maryland: 1988), "Hollywood Grand: A Look at Wyoming's Movie Theaters between the years 1900-1950," delineates where and when theaters opened in Wyoming.

"Country School Legacy in Wyoming" an article written by Andrew Guilford appeared in *Annals of Wyoming* Fall 1982 (Volume 42, No. 2).

Energy Development

Three historic overviews and one master's thesis offer general information about the oil industry in Wyoming. "Historic Evaluation of Kyle Oil Camp, Carbon County, Wyoming" written by Dudley Gardner and David Johnson, Archaeological Services, Western Wyoming College (May 1986), "Historic Overview of the LaBarge Gas and Oil Field, Lincoln and Sublette Counties, Wyoming" written by Dudley Gardner, David Johnson and Ted Hoefer III of Archaeological Services, Western Wyoming College (December 1990) and the "Historic Overview of the Salt Creek Oil Field, Natrona County, Wyoming" written by Robert Rosenberg in March 1988 all offer detailed information about energy development history. William Metz wrote his unpublished master's thesis, "The Historical Archaeology of the Oil and Gas Industry in Wyoming" for Ball State University in June 1986 which is quite informative.

Two books published recently do not specifically deal with architecture yet offer valuable information about coal mining in Wyoming and surrounding states. These books, *Regulating Danger: The Struggle for Mine Safety in the Rocky Mountain Coal Industry* written by James Whiteside (Lincoln: University of Nebraska, 1990) and *Forgotten Frontier: A History of Wyoming Coal Mining* by Dudley Gardner and Verla R. Flores (Boulder: Westview Press, 1989), add significant information to mining history.

Government Buildings

Lois Craig, editor, and the staff of the Federal Architecture Project wrote *The Federal Presence: Architecture, Politics, and Symbols in the United States Government Building* (Cambridge, Massachusetts: M.I.T. Press, 1979) which discusses the theory and motivation in federal architecture.

Military

Architectural Survey: F. E. Warren Air Force Base, a multi-volume set, assembled by the Air Force Regional

Civil Engineer-Ballistic Missile Support and its consultant URS Burger in 1984 was previously mentioned and has a great deal of information about F. E. Warren Air Force Base.

Railroad Architecture

The Country Railroad Station in America by H. Roger Grant and Charles W. Bohi (Boulder: Pruett Publishing Company, 1978) offers architectural information about different types of country railroad stations. An unpublished article, "The Historic Railroad Building of Albuquerque: an Assessment of Significance" written by Chris Wilson, August 1986, offers information on New Mexico buildings with parallels that can be drawn to Wyoming.

Religious Architecture

Jeannie Cook of Park County shared information on the community of Germania/Emblem. There is a profound need for further work and study in the area of religious architecture of the Rocky Mountain West.

Residential

Numerous books discuss residential architecture; some have already been mentioned. A general guide to American residential structures was written by Virginia and Lee McAlester, *A Field Guide to American Houses* (New York: Alfred A. Knopf, 1984).

Tourism

Main Street to Miracle Mile: America's Roadside Architecture by Chester Liebs is a classic examination of roadside architecture (Boston: Little, Brown, 1985).

"A Sense of Shelter: Robert C. Reamer in Yellowstone National Park" written by David Leavengood and published in the *Pacific Historical Review*, November 1985, (Volume LIV, Number 4) explores Robert Reamer's life. "Architecture in the Parks: National Historic Landmark Theme Study" by Laura Soulliere Harrison, of the National Park Service, Department of the Interior, prepared in 1986, discusses architecture in Yellowstone. *Park and Recreation Structures* by Albert Good, National Park Service, written in 1938 is a rich source of information about specific structures and the Park Service's philosophy on rustic architecture. Another informative document produced by the Park Service, "National Park Service Rustic Architecture: 1916-1942" written by William C. Tweed, Laura E. Soulliere, Henry G. Law, of the NPS Western Regional Office, (February 1977) also explores park architecture.

Dude Ranching: A Complete History by Lawrence Bourne (Albuquerque: University of New Mexico Press, 1983) details Wyoming and the Rocky Mountain West's dude ranching history. *Crucible for Conservation: The Creation of Grand Teton National Park* by Robert W. Righter (Colorado Associated University Press, 1982) is an interesting history of Grand Teton National Park.

Ch. 6-Preserving Wyoming's Buildings

The State Historic Preservation Office has numerous free publications on a variety of historic preservation topics. For information about historic preservation in Wyoming, contact the SHPO/Department of Commerce, Barrett Building, Cheyenne, WY 82002. For a copy of *Wyoming's Comprehensive Historic Preservation Plan* also contact the SHPO.

The National Trust for Historic Preservation is the largest grass-roots preservation organization in the United States. For more information about membership or information on books that are available contact: National Trust for Historic Preservation, 1785 Massachusetts Avenue, N.W., Washington D.C. 20036.

Index